# Healing Hearts

*Helping Children and Adults Recover from Divorce*

Elizabeth Hickey, MSW
*Family Counselor and Mediator*

*and*

Elizabeth A. Dalton, J.D.
*Attorney and Mediator*

GOLD LEAF PRESS

Healing Hearts

© 1994 Elizabeth Hickey, Elizabeth Dalton

All rights reserved

Printed in the United States of America

No portion of this book may be reproduced in any form
without written permission from the publisher.
Gold Leaf Press, 2533 North Carson St., Suite 1544,
Carson City, NV  89706
1-800-748-4900

Library of Congress Cataloging-in-Publication Data

Hickey, Elizabeth
Healing Hearts: Helping Children and Adults Recover from Divorce
by Elizabeth Hickey, Elizabeth Dalton.
p.  cm.
ISBN 1-882723-11-2 : $19.95
1. Children of divorced parents—United States—Psychology.
2. Divorced parents—United States—Psychology.  3. Parenting, Part-time—United
States.  4. Divorce—United States.  5. Divorce—United States—Psychological aspects.  I.
Dalton, Elizabeth.  II. Title.
HQ777.5.H53 1994

306.89–dc20                                                                                          94-3618
                                                                                                          CIP

*Dedicated to the children of*
*divorce who shared their pain, so*
*we could discover the pathways*
*to healing hearts*

# Acknowledgments

First and foremost we must acknowledge and thank the Spirit that inspired us to help heal the hearts of those who have suffered wounds . . . our peace comes from knowing that we are all indeed connected by a power and presence greater than ourselves, and this force can and will inspire the good to rise within each and every one of us. Thus, we are all united through love.

We also appreciate the continual and dedicated support from Terina Darcey, an outstanding person committed to reminding others of the truth within them, her dedication to typing, revisions, and edits will always be remembered and cherished. Additionally, we thank Dawn Hall Anderson, Charlotte Romney Howe, Janet Bernice, Darla Isackson, and Steve Romney who worked tenaciously at improving the manuscript, and who also allowed the spirit of the project to guide them. Our gratitude is also extended to Rebecca Ryser, Ph.D. whose clinical insights into this manuscript were invaluable.

Elizabeth Hickey: I thank my daughter Aimee, her honesty of heart teaches me well; and my former husband, Gifford, who joined me in self-discovery as we progressed through our marriage and our divorce.

Elizabeth Dalton: I thank my parents, my children, and my former husband for the insights they gave me on my own journey of healing.

# Table of Contents

# About the Book

Divorce is a major life change. It inevitably involves strong emotions, but also offers an opportunity for self-examination and individual growth. One goal of *Healing Hearts* is to help you seize that opportunity.

Chapters of the book dealing with interpersonal issues and individual growth were written by Elizabeth Hickey, MSW. As a family counselor, child custody evaluator, and divorce mediator, Ms. Hickey leads you through the personal processes of divorce and highlights the things you can do to help you and your child make a healthy adjustment to the situation.

To obtain a divorce in our country, it is necessary to enter the legal system. Unless one is familiar with the legal divorce process, it can be very confusing and unsettling. Therefore, a secondary goal of *Healing Hearts* is to take the mystery out of the legal process.

When you understand the legal options available to you, the process of your divorce will be less frustrating, and you will have more control of the outcome. Guiding you through the legal intricacies of divorce in Chapters 12, 13, 14 and 15, of *Healing Hearts* is Elizabeth Dalton, J.D., who is an attorney and divorce mediator.

The third contributor to *Healing Hearts* was a group of children. As this book was being written, we were also working on a video project entitled, *Children: The Experts on Divorce.* We interviewed over fifty children about how their parents' divorce affected them. Then the children provided advice to parents about how to make divorce easier on other children. Their words of wisdom are shared throughout the book. Their names have been changed to protect the sensitive nature of the parent-child relationship.

We are especially grateful to the children, who openly shared their most vulnerable feelings so that others might learn. If we listen, the children can teach us well.


All poems, song lyrics, and sidebar quotes were written by Elizabeth Hickey unless otherwise noted.

# Introduction

This book was written primarily to help you support your children through your divorce, but another important goal is to help your heart heal from the emotional and romantic wounds it has suffered. In order for you to be the best possible parent to your child, the wounds in your heart require healing.

Just as a heart surgeon can only repair the physical aspects of a heart ailment, the court is only a means for parents to finalize their divorce. The doctor, the court, or the lawyer cannot be responsible for healing wounds. Healing can only be done by the person suffering the wound. Others may come along and assist the healing process, but ultimately, the responsibility for healing the wound rests with the individual. For that to happen, hearts need to be open to the various possibilities for healing, which may take place in the form of therapy, spiritual assistance, going within, support groups, friends, or books. Whatever you do, it is most important that you open yourself up to the necessary process for healing your heart.

Healing the wounds of the past will enable both you and your child to move forward with your lives. In love, we share these words with you hoping they will inspire you to embrace the opportunity. Remember that many other divorcing parents have experienced similar depths of emotion. They have not only "gotten through it," but many have also used the opportunity to take significant steps in their emotional and spiritual growth. That same opportunity awaits you.

We wish you and your family well.

# Part I

by Elizabeth Hickey, MSW

Deer Mommy,

Whear are you.

I miss you

Do you miss me.

Do you love me

Do you think

good. mommy I am

right back. plees

we love you

# 1

# *Healing Broken Hearts*

Emily is five years old and her parents are getting divorced. Her father left a month ago and her world has been turned upside down. Her mother has been constantly bad-mouthing her father, which hurts Emily's feelings. Now they have to move out of their home and live with Emily's grandparents. Emily doesn't understand what is going on. She misses her father. She misses her mother's reassuring voice. Frightened and confused, Emily is crying herself to sleep at night. Her parents, though well-intentioned, don't know what to tell her or how to say it. They are both hurt and confused, too, and feel that their hopes and dreams have been shattered.

The pain within this family is felt by relatives, neighbors, and friends. Unless this pain is acknowledged and resolved, it will turn to anger. We see the anger manifested in our communities every time we turn on the evening news.

It is time to stop the crime, the anger, and the hurt. It is time to start healing hearts all across the country. Our future depends on healthy hearts. Our future depends on all of us helping to heal the pain.

We need to help each other through the challenges and transitions we face, for we are all in this world together. Healing broken hearts is the responsibility of all.

At this challenging crossroads, America is struggling with many social problems that can be traced back to the breakdown

In every community, there is work to be done. In every nation, there are wounds to heal. In every heart, there is the power to do it.
—Marianne
    Williamson
*A Return To Love*
*(Harper-Collins)*

of the family unit. For better or for worse, divorce as an option in our society, is here to stay. We may be able to create preventive programs that could reduce the almost 50 percent divorce rate, but even if that is done, we must still deal with the fallout from the past three decades that produced millions of children who experienced their parents' divorce.

There is no question that divorces can be done better in our country. Divorce is an emotional and psychological experience. Many hurting adults who are in the process of divorce try to use the legal system to resolve their emotional pains. *Healing Hearts: Helping Children and Adults Recover From Divorce* promotes a greater understanding of the complexity of the issues involved when two parents get divorced. It is a comprehensive manual addressing the psychological aspects of divorce, as well as answering legal questions.

Each year, over one million children in the United States face their parents' divorce. This issue demands much greater attention than it's been getting because a child's adjustment to a divorce is directly related to how the divorce is handled. As a country, we should be doing everything in our power to help parents manage divorce better for the sake of millions of children.

Collectively we need to reexamine how we handle matters related to the heart. We need a system that provides an avenue for healing—not for perpetuating conflict. Change can occur when people get the vision that it is possible to change. Our children need us to have that vision.

*Healing Hearts* provides healthy alternatives to the current adversarial system that parents are thrust into when they initiate a divorce. It offers information that will help parents, children, and other extended family members achieve a more "family friendly" divorce by encouraging emotional connection within families. Our goal is to empower divorcing parents through

The earth does not belong to man, man belongs to the earth. . . . Man did not weave the web of life, he is merely a strand in it. Whatever he does to the web, he does to himself.

— Chief Seattle

acknowledging the reality of their painful situation and providing information about their options for handling their divorce. And ultimately, hearts will be healed.

Since July 1992, more than 10,000 parents have been required to attend the Divorce Education Course for Parents in Utah. At the end of the class, we ask the parents to complete a class evaluation, and the results are compiled by court personnel. We have found that although most parents are initially reluctant to attend the class—most are even resentful—an overwhelming majority have revised their opinion by the end of the class.

The chart on the next page is a compilation of what the first 3,360 parents said about the course.

After teaching divorce education classes (both voluntary and mandatory) for nearly three years, we have learned what over 10,000 parents wanted to know about divorce. (We learned even more from firsthand experience in our own divorces.) As parents begin to understand their children's needs, they can make the choices that will support them through this difficult time.

Our goal has been to make divorce less traumatic for both children and parents. We kept that goal uppermost in our minds while we worked on this book. We believe the information we are sharing will encourage a stronger and healthier bond between you and your child, particularly as you go through your divorce.

I am not concerned that you have fallen. I am concerned that you arise.
—Abraham Lincoln

Never doubt that a small group of thoughtful, committed citizens can change the world; indeed it's the only thing that ever has.
—Margaret Mead

# Evaluation Results for Mandatory Divorce Education for Parents Course (9/93)

| | | |
|---|---|---|
| 76% | Agree | I resented having to attend this course. |
| 89% | Agree | In spite of this, I felt the course worthwhile. |
| 77% | Agree | I think the course should be mandatory for all divorcing parents. |
| 92% | Agree | The course helped me to understand how children are affected by divorce. |
| 86% | Agree | The information presented will have an influence on the decisions I make regarding my children. |
| 90% | Agree | Although I may not feel like cooperating with my ex-spouse, I now understand why it is important to do so. |
| 88% | Agree | I plan to make a stronger effort to work with my ex-spouse for the children's sake. |
| 87% | Agree | As a result, I am most likely to utilize a time-sharing plan that allows both parents to have a meaningful relationship with the children. |

# 2
# *Why Shared Parenting?*

There are many reasons divorcing parents should establish a plan to share the parenting of their children. The most important is that every child deserves the *opportunity* to have a meaningful, healthy relationship with both parents. A child needs to feel free to love both parents, as well as to be loved by both.

Parents should cooperate to make the process of divorce easier for their child. After all, it is the parents' conflict, not the child's. Children often feel as if they need to take sides in a conflict, yet it is impossible to be on both sides.

I have seen the pain of children who live in confusion because of their parents' divorce. Their anxiety is made worse by their feeling powerless to change anything. Often they cannot even tell their parents how much it hurts to be caught in their struggles. Afraid of upsetting their parents, wanting to protect them, children rarely say more than, "Please, don't fight."

Although it is healthy to be honest about your painful emotions during your divorce, expressing how you feel should take place in the presence of a friend or therapist—not in the presence of your children who will always have an independent relationship with your ex-partner.

Both relationships are part of the child's identity, and to disrupt the bond between a child and either mother or father is traumatic. The human need to feel connected to both parents becomes especially critical if the parents are divorcing. When one

I think parents should tell kids that they love them and they shouldn't play tug of war with them because that is how I felt when my parents got divorced. Like, one of them would say, "Do you like me or her?" I wouldn't know what to say. I would love both of them and both of them had their faults and their great things about them. I just wish I wasn't stuck in the middle of them.
—Tawnya, age 11

parent prevents the other from having access to a child, the trauma of divorce is magnified.

The losses of divorce are enormous for everyone. Children need both parents' support to help them through. Because you love your children, you want what is best for them. What is best for them is a healthy relationship with both parents, and they need permission from each parent to enjoy a relationship with the other.

But that permission is hard to give. In one study (see Chapter 3), 80 percent of the children who had experienced divorce showed evidence of being "brainwashed" to think less of one parent by the other parent. Parents, perhaps subconsciously wishing to be justified in their child's eyes, will often subtly pressure a child to choose sides. Consider the emotional conflict this pressure inflicts on children. They need the freedom to love each of their parents. Not having that freedom is a no-win situation. The child cannot please both parents without lying about feelings and loyalties. When children lie to protect a parent's feelings, they will inevitably feel guilty for being disloyal. Anyway you look at it, taking sides in a parent's conflict causes unnecessary stress for a child.

Another factor which increases the stress of divorce is timing. In most cases, individuals do not arrive at the decision to divorce simultaneously. Usually, one partner decides to seek a divorce. The other partner feels the pain of rejection and suffers intensely. This pain often motivates a desire to retaliate. Divorce spawns horror stories of people reacting to pain without considering the consequences. For their children's sake, parents need to separate emotional pain from the rational process of supporting a child's needs. Acknowledging that children's needs are different from the parents' is a big first step.

Children need to feel secure. Parental conflicts during divorce

> Parents should give their kids a chance to tell them that they love you, but they love the other one too and it is kind of hard when one of them is saying how rotten the other one is. You are saying that you love both of them and it creates a gap between your parents and you.
>
> —Megan, age 12

leave a child feeling frightened, insecure, and powerless. Many studies, in fact, show that the extent of parental conflict is the major factor in how a child will psychologically adjust to divorce. Conflict creates fear, and no one feels trust or security in the presence of fear. Most children hold their fear and pain in, but eventually that fear and pain need to be released. At times the stress children feel may manifest itself in the form of a physical illness.

I try to make them happy so they aren't mad no more.

—Jason, age 5

*This child explained that he could hear his parents' fights through the heating vent.*

Some years ago, I was interviewing Sandy, age ten, as part of a child custody evaluation. In my office, Sandy had been describing her parents' fights when suddenly she began crying so hard that she was shaking. I held her for twenty minutes while she sobbed. No words were spoken; none were necessary. She simply needed to release the pain of being in the middle of her parents' battle. I visited Sandy several weeks later in her hospital room following surgery to remove a cancerous tumor. While still under medication

Children caught in the middle will inevitably feel guilty for switching loyalties, depending on the parent they are with. This will not enable them to feel peace. Most likely, they will end up feeling resentment toward both parents for putting them in this difficult situation.

from the surgery, she said to me, "I just need a rest. Do you think I could stay here for a while?" Tired of the tug-of-war, she longed for peace, for a time-out from the battle. The hospital seemed to provide a safe haven. Sandy's parents loved her with all their hearts, but they had not made the connection between their fights and Sandy's stress. Eventually, they did, but it had to be strongly pointed out to them.

Parenting, with all its rewards, requires many sacrifices. During and after divorce, children need parents to continue making sacrifices, especially by not drawing them into the battle and by respecting the child's relationship with the other parent. What else can you do to support them in the aftermath of divorce? You can make decisions that are clearly motivated from the desire to create peace for your child.

## Our Personal Stories

I had been working in the human services field for ten years. As I dealt with hundreds of parents and children who were struggling with heartfelt pain, I always felt deep empathy. In 1989 I was even awarded the "Outstanding Public Employee of the Year" for my empathetic approach.

But little of the work prepared me for the pain I felt when my own marriage ended in divorce. My husband, Gifford, and I had years of problems that had accumulated without resolution. Eventually, that frustration resulted in the decision to divorce. We obtained a legal divorce but then tried reconciling for two more years. We had one child together, Aimee. We agreed to joint legal custody and to cooperate on parenting issues. Before I reacted to my pain, I gave it a lot of thought.

In my practice I had seen people who once loved each other do horrible things to one another, in one case hiring a hit man to kill a former spouse. When a relationship ends, there is enough

It is hard when people get divorces.
—Lisa, age 7

pain and disappointment to go around, without adding more.

Many adults draw the children into the conflict as a weapon to wound the other person. They ignore or forget that this other person is still a parent to the children—and always will be. Once the children have been drawn into the conflict to hurt the former spouse, getting back to a place of forgiveness and rational choices is tremendously difficult. But it is still possible and very important to acknowledge the error and get back on the path of forgiveness.

Knowing all of this, I usually chose to cooperate with Giff, even when doing so didn't coincide with what I was feeling. Keeping my emotions from clouding my common sense was very difficult, but I knew it was necessary. I had to make a point of checking my motives often.

At times my pain was so great that I wanted to hurt my former husband for the way he had hurt me. It hurt to be rejected. It was extremely difficult to watch him go off and be with another woman. It would have been easy to try to get back at him through my child. But I knew that this was a critical point where many divorcing adults make their most far-reaching mistakes. Hurting each other through the children disrupts everyone's future. When the children become involved, it is difficult to end the cycle of retribution and retaliation.

Through it all, my husband and I argued with each other about every other aspect of our relationship. But we never fought over our child. Without ever formally agreeing to this boundary, we both knew this turf was off limits, and we fought around it.

We've always had joint legal custody, with my home being the primary residence. Gifford wanted out of the marital relationship, but did not want to hurt Aimee. He felt protective toward her. As he moved into a new life with someone else, he wanted to see that Aimee and I were comfortable. Although it may have been his initial guilt that prompted him, I will always be grateful to

> We are not very much to blame for our bad marriages. . . In the worst assorted connections there is ever some mixture of true marriage.
> —Ralph Waldo Emerson

Is it possible to have a peaceful parting when these are matters of the heart?

Emotions know no sense.

They feel.
They break.
They suffocate.

Can we send them somewhere else while we have a peaceful parting?

him for this. Once some of the bitterness subsided, I could also look for opportunities to express my appreciation to him. Most recently I was able to surprise him with two tickets to take Aimee to Seattle to visit with his sister and her family. Taking my own advice proved easier to say than to do, but the results have been worth the effort.

Through the process of extending acts of kindness to each other, our hearts were softened. We learned to exchange many favors and in the process, we began to see each other as resources and not obstacles. If either of us had held onto the anger and blaming, we would still feel miserable, as would everyone around us. Since that approach serves no one, we forgave each other and ourselves, and moved forward to new lives and new relationships.

One special relationship is the maturing love I see between Aimee and her father. The love between Gifford and Aimee has been beautiful and touching to watch. I could never do anything to hurt that. It brings me joy to watch them interact in their own special, separate way. Aimee feels the depth of her father's love, in addition to mine. Because of this, she will never question her lovability, and in this she is fortunate.

I asked my former husband, Gifford, as well as Elizabeth Dalton (co-author) and her former husband, Don, to write briefly about co-parenting and divorce. Our purpose is to give hope and encouragement to other parents struggling with their divorces and feelings for their children.

## *Always a Father* by *Gifford Hickey*

As with any radical change in one's life, divorce draws forth feelings that take you from one end of the emotional pole to the other. With years of love, hate, happiness, confusion, and contentment all wrapped into what feels like a flash, I had to ask "Why divorce?"

After ten years of marriage and two years of being divorced, I am still not totally content with the answers I came up with. Maybe I'll never be, but I know it is the right decision for now.

One's love for a friend, lover, companion, former wife does not vanish with the stroke of a pen. It becomes a memory and for me, a lesson. Our marriage was a path, an experience which I hope will push the boundaries of what little I know of love. I will always hold a place in my heart for Elizabeth. For me what happened was meant to be—our meeting, our marriage, and our parting. I can only thank her for all she has taught me.

As for Aimee, Elizabeth and I know of the love we each have for our precious child. I was blessed with a sweet daughter who makes my eyes shine bright and my heart soar. She is the heart of my life, the reason for each breath I take. I could never express in words my love for her. It comes from the deepest part of my soul and flows through me like blood.

In the meantime, I know time and life are my teachers, and I patiently wait for the next chapter. There is a purpose for everything.

## Shared Parenting Is Possible *by Elizabeth Dalton*

I married when I was twenty—an idealistic college sophomore, full of dreams of family life and children. My husband, Don, was about to start law school in Los Angeles. As a young bride, I ventured out from my childhood home to create a home of my own. Don and I spent nine years "growing up together," getting our law degrees, setting up practices in Salt Lake City, and bringing two beautiful children into this world.

Although Don and I started our family anticipating marital success and joy, we both underwent personal changes in philosophy and religion that resulted in my decision to end our marriage.

> A new philosophy, a way of life, is not given for nothing. It has to be paid dearly for and only acquired with much patience and great effort.
> —Fyodor Dostoyevsky

That decision caught Don, and even me, off guard.

I could not have predicted the range of emotions we experienced. I remember crying for two weeks straight and being "out of it" at work for months. Don and our two daughters were generally "shell-shocked." Some days we were sad; other days we were angry. At our lowest point, with both of us feeling angry, confused, and unable to deal with the situation rationally, I drove off to a hotel in my mini-van with our two children.

Luckily for our children, as attorneys we both knew the potentially disastrous consequences of divorce litigation on a family. We made one of the most important decisions of our lives. We decided to put aside our personal differences and focus on the needs of our children. Don and I created from scratch a post divorce co-parenting relationship. At the time we divorced in 1990, the concept of shared parenting was relatively new in Utah.

During the process of our divorce, I attended a week of divorce mediation training taught by CDR Associates in Boulder, Colorado. What I learned was revolutionary and has affected my entire life. I incorporated many of the principles I learned into my own divorce. I then opened one of the first divorce mediation practices in Salt Lake City, Utah.

During the past four years, Don and I have built and fortified a constructive and resourceful co-parenting relationship. We work together as "business partners," motivated to help each other achieve the mutual goal of raising our two girls to be well-adjusted and successful in life. We have changed our time-sharing arrangement three times, increased communication, involved in-laws and Don's new wife, and have successfully created two supportive homes for our children.

Friends and family have stood back bewildered at our successful co-parenting relationship. They see us talking, laughing, and communicating freely. They see us sharing time with our children, along with decision-making and child-raising responsibilities. From time to time, I go shopping with Don's new wife. (It stills shocks us both that we do this!) We trade babysitting for each other. We have birthday parties together. We save seats and sit together at school programs. My children call their stepmother "Mom" with my support and can call my new husband "Dad" with Don's support.

We focus on the abundance of opportunities for love rather than loyalty battles and love competitions. Most of my friends and family members have only seen "broken" families and embittered parents after a divorce. What they see in my life is a restructured family. To many, it looks like a miracle.

Nevertheless, this miracle did not happen overnight. Our co-parenting style has emerged through a trial and error process. Although we settled our divorce in two weeks, before long we had differences which landed us back in court. After slinging mud back and forth for a while, we got back on track when we realized how much of our girls' lives we were missing while we focused our energies on futile fights. We recommitted ourselves to co-parenting.

We have overlooked many mistakes, discourtesies, and misunderstandings and have been willing to start over and try again. Our commitment to co-parenting has sustained us and given us the hope that we can make shared parenting a reality.

From my own experience, I have come to understand the power of personal choice. Every choice has a consequence. The choice Don and I made four years ago to become co-parents has resulted in our children "making it" despite the traumatic event of divorce. My children are happy. In the eyes of their school teachers they are well adjusted and at the top of their classes academically.

Recently, I realized how significant my choice to become a co-parent was. While at the playground with my two daughters, I overheard my oldest daughter, Sara, age ten, talking to a friend.

*I'm happy because my parents had a good divorce.*
— Sara Dalton, age 10

I heard her explaining how she had a home with her dad and a home with her mom. Most important, I heard her say, "I'm happy because my parents had a good divorce."

We chose to make a miracle happen in our family. This book is written to show you how to make a miracle happen in your family as well.

## Co-Parenting: Living for Your Children  *by Don Dalton*

Co-parenting through separation and divorce will test the mettle of the strongest parent. If you're on the receiving end of the separation or divorce announcement, you will likely experience an "end-of-the-world" type of reaction, "Is she/he taking my children away? Will I ever see them again? Things will never be the way they were."

And they never will be. Every person, even the one on the delivery end, will have to deal with an awful reality. Things will not be the same. There is going to be a vastly different set of circumstances that are both complicated and emotionally supercharged.

The test is to rise above this devastation and in the bargain rise above yourself. When my ex-wife and I separated and ultimately divorced, we promised to put our anger on a shelf, at least when it came to dealing with our kids. We promised to talk each other up to the kids. We made sure, as much as possible, that they never saw the anger and disappointment kindling in our hearts.

I remember all this as kind of a blur. I wanted to lash out, and I wanted her to feel my anger. I would not have been above using the kids to get at my intended target, except that I recognized the truth of the proposition. Divorce is hard enough on the kids. Why make it harder? Letting them have my anger would hurt them more than my ex-wife. Co-parenting became an exercise in exceeding tolerance and self-discipline. I'm sure I was not perfect. But every time they asked me if I still cared about Mommy, I could report, although through gritted teeth, that "Yes, indeed I did."

The proof was in the pudding. We went to see a psychological counselor together, and were told that the kids were adjusting

extremely well to the separation and divorce. Not that they were happy with the situation—but taking them out of our equation allowed them to do separation and anxiety work free from the restraints of parental loyalty.

The answer is that kids can work through the grief and anger incident to divorce and separation. But they can't do it if they are dealing with guilt and anxiety—feelings pressed on them by a parent consumed with anger toward a former spouse.

That is the beginning. As soon as you start dealing with the anger, hurt, pain, and grief, it is time to face another emotional milestone. You live for your children, not the other way around. I have an interesting philosophy: Bringing children into the world is one of the most selfish things a human can do. When we think about bringing children into the world (assuming we think before we do it), we do not do it to make them happy. I believe we bring them into the world because we believe they will make us happy. And then their happiness becomes a concern to us, because if they aren't happy, we aren't happy.

Divorce and separation turns all of this around. Suddenly, you are confronted with the proposition: "Do I live for them, or do I make them live for me?" You need emotional support through the divorce process, and it becomes very easy to use the children. Children can become great empathizers and are very good at consoling and loving a hurt and grieving parent. The problem is, you are taking something from them that does not belong to you. Their happiness is paramount; you have to get yours somewhere else.

This became clearer for me further down the road. At first, we had a 50/50 custodial arrangement. I thought it was great. After a while, I began to wonder if it was what the kids wanted. As they grew older, I saw that they chafed under the system. As they established deeper roots, they needed less from me than before. What they needed was to spend more time at "home." My girls needed a "primary home," a place they can spend most of their time.

I was not entirely happy to see that someone was going to lose. I still seethe at the notion, but I could see that this someone had to be me. I am now a weekend father (except in the summers). I am not thrilled about this, but this is the bottom line: I think the children are happier. When I honestly assess my feelings, that is what I really want. That thought makes it easier.

Co-parenting is not about the quantity of time a parent spends with their children. It is about knowing and showing interest in what's going on in the lives of your children. It's about listening to their problems, knowing about their teachers, friends, pets, activities, and other things.

Kids tell you what's going on in their lives, not so you can give them advice. They do it because they want your approval. (Was it different when you were a kid?) Someday—who knows when—you may be the one they turn to in a crisis. They may do this precisely because you are not the one in the middle of it. In order for this to happen, you have to be available for them. Be in the picture, not overshadowing it. They'll appreciate you for doing this.

It is important to take a step back and reflect on what type of relationship you want to create with your child's other parent. True commitment to a co-parenting relationship can make it happen.

---

## The Power of Commitment

*Until one is committed, there is hesitancy,*
*the chance to draw back, always ineffectiveness.*

*Concerning all acts of initiative and creation,*
*there is one elementary truth, the ignorance of which*
*kills countless ideas and splendid plans:*

*The moment one definitely commits oneself,*
*then Providence moves too.*

*All sorts of things occur to help one that would never*
*otherwise have occurred.*

*A whole stream of events issues from the decision,*
*raising in one's favor all manner of*
*unforeseen incidents and meetings*
*and material assistance,*
*which no man could have dreamed*
*would have come his way.*

*Whatever you can do,*
*or dream you can,*
*begin it.*

*Boldness has genius, power and magic in it.*
*Begin it now.*

— *Goethe*

# 3
# *In the Eyes of a Child*

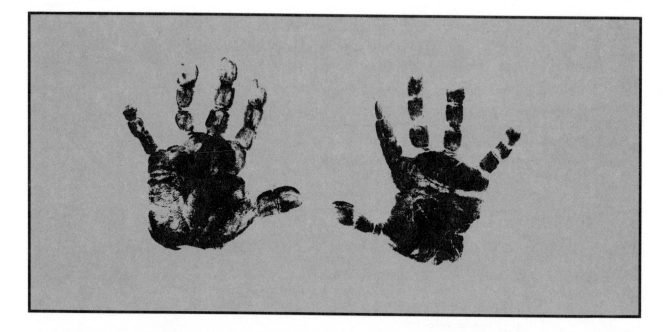

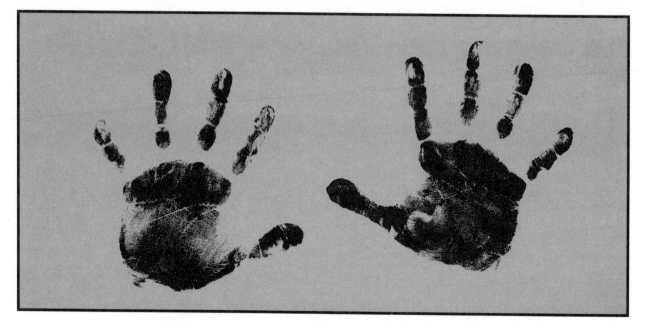

# Children Need Parents Who Remember

*When I was born*
*I was precious*
*My parents knew*
*Just what I needed to coo and smile.*

*When I was two*
*I still needed hugs and cuddles*
*But there was also a new baby*
*Who needed lots of attention.*

*When I was four*
*I wondered about the*
*Mysterious world of adults*
*Words and letters were a secret language*
*And I felt left out.*

*When I was six*
*I still needed to cry*
*But I was told to*
*Be a "big girl" now.*

*When I was eight*
*I was confused about*
*Things adults said*
*But I was afraid to say anything.*

*When I was ten*
*I needed to know*
*My parents still loved me*
*But I felt too big to ask for a hug.*

*When I was twelve*
*I cried myself to sleep*
*Because I felt alone*
*But didn't know how to reach out.*

*When I was fourteen*
*I didn't know how to*
*Cope with peer pressure*
*But I didn't want to admit it.*

*When I was sixteen*
*I needed to belong in the world*
*I was trying out new ways to fit in*
*My family thought I was weird.*

*When I was eighteen*
*I moved away*
*I felt sad and scared*
*But I needed to act strong.*

*Now that I'm a parent*
*My child needs me*
*To remember how it felt*
*To be a child.*

Children need to see that their parents understand how it feels to be a child. Every day you have the opportunity to increase and reinforce your child's feelings of self-worth. As you go through the divorce, it is of particular importance that you keep these things in mind. Much of your energy will be consumed in merely coping with the changes and stress that divorce brings on.

Children of divorce have collectively and independently made comments concerning the reduced amount of positive attention they receive from their parents during and after the divorce. They simply notice that they're not hearing as many positive, friendly comments during the stress of divorce. Unfortunately, many children interpret this to mean that the parent doesn't love them as much anymore. This is a precise example of how a child misinterprets things that are going on around him. But such misinterpretation can be avoided merely by anticipating it and taking steps to prevent it. Recognizing that children of all ages need support on a regular basis in the following areas, helps your child make a healthier adjustment to your divorce.

## Trust

When a child knows her needs will be provided for, she feels safe. When she knows she can trust the people in her environment, she is secure and well-adjusted. As a parent, you earn a child's trust when she compares your words with your actions and finds them congruent. During divorce, trust is something that is challenged for adults as well as children. The mere fact that you can no longer count on the promises that were exchanged when you married, which you trusted would bring you happiness, hurts your ability to trust. When betrayal or rejection enters into the picture, you will need time to trust again. But when you're feeling a lack of trust in your world, your child will pick up on those feelings. The trust that she needs to gain from you during this tough time lies in the reality that you will be there for her and that her needs will be taken care of, both emotionally and physically. When she believes this, she feels safe and trust remains intact.

---

### Nurturing the Innocence of the Child Spirit

*The child spirit can endure*
*But it needs to feel secure*
*If innocence is to survive*

*We need to pull together*
*And persevere the weather*
*The storms will come and pass*

*But for our child,*
*Trust and love*
*is what should last.*

---

## Communication

Children of all ages need to understand what is happening around them. Talking and explaining takes the guessing out of what might or could happen. Talking about how important your children are to you provides them a solid foundation and a great deal of comfort.

Communication often tends to decrease during divorce. Parents can look for opportunities to connect with their children. Children of divorce tell us that they have lots of questions as family members become preoccupied trying to cope with consequent changes and emotions. They also say they won't approach their parents and start talking about divorce because they're not sure how to do it. They worry about upsetting a parent by saying the wrong thing. Many children see a whole new range of emotions and behaviors that they've never seen before, displayed by their parents. This is unsettling for them. Therefore, parents should initiate communication when it comes to the topic of divorce.

## Listening

Being listened to makes any child feel validated and important—feelings which build self-esteem. Caring enough to step out of your adult world and connect with your children can have a powerful effect. You are showing your children how very much you value them when you take the time to listen to their perceptions of the world.

As parents we usually listen to our children from a "protective" position. As caretakers and guardians, parents want to protect, offer insight, and shield their children from pain. Sometimes, these good intentions are the very things that stand in the way of developing good listening skills. Many concerned parents develop a style of responding to their child by giving advice, offering a solution, or making an interpretation. What children really want is to be heard. They want to know that their parents care enough to simply listen. Listening is one of the strongest tools we have available to us as parents for strengthening the bond with our children. Children of divorce emphasize over and over how important it is for parents to listen to how the divorce feels for them.

## Honesty

Providing honest explanations of what goes on during a divorce is a challenge for any parent, but it is a crucial time for you to cautiously share the truth. By not giving in to the temptation to distort the situation or to encourage your child to take sides, you are rebuilding the foundation of trust between the two of you.

Parents should just listen to what their kids are saying and not try to talk them out of how they are feeling. My parents used to try and convince me that my feelings were wrong and theirs were right. All that did was push me away from them. When I tried to tell them this, they just did the same thing and told me that I was wrong. How can someone be wrong for what they are feeling? They didn't have a clue they were doing this either.

—Randy, age 15

> *Gentle truth shared with a*
> *nonjudgmental attitude,*
> *respects a child's freedom*
> *to trust*
> *their knowing eyes.*

## Consistency

When there is consistency in a child's world, they learn what they can count on. A sense of predictability creates feelings of security. Sometimes the differences of divorcing parents get exaggerated in the process of divorcing. A common problem in divorce occurs when the custodial parent feels they have all the responsibility for enforcing rules, such as reasonable bedtime, homework, baths, and so on.

On the other hand, the noncustodial parent often feels their time with the child is so limited, that they want to pack in the fun to create good memories. Since it is often weekend time, a reasonable bedtime doesn't seem important, and homework can wait.

In both scenarios, there are obvious differences in the lifestyle the child experiences in the two homes. While some consistency in rules and expectations between homes is beneficial to a child, they can also learn to understand the different style of each of their parents if the differences are not too far apart.

Explaining why there are differences makes it easier for the child to accept them. Try a statement such as "You know, Nancy, that when you come over here to my house, I let you stay up later because you don't have school the next day and you can sleep in in the morning. But when you're at your dad's house, he makes you go to bed at 8:30 because it's important to get a good night's rest before school. I agree with that. If you lived at my house during the week, I would do the same thing." This type of statement shows support for the other parent and decreases the likelihood that the child will play one parent against the other.

## Developmental Stages and Divorce

Children progress through distinct stages in development. At each stage, there are goals to be reached if the child is to move with confidence to the next stage.

Interference with normal development may come from insecurity or changes in normal procedures, surroundings, and caregivers. Unfortunately, all of these anxieties are inherent in divorce. If divorcing parents are sensitive to these challenges, the opportunity for increased growth and greater flexibility can await the child.

All children, regardless of age, are affected by divorce. When parents are aware of the challenges and behaviors typical of each developmental stage of their children, they can better meet their needs and help their children through difficult times.

## "I Know You . . . I Trust You"

### Birth to Age 1

### Description

As any parent has experienced, trust comes naturally to a cherished infant. A baby will normally build strong emotional bonds with her caregivers. Familiarity and consistency are very important at this stage because they give a child the strength and confidence needed to start exploring the world.

### Divorce Anxiety

Changes in environment and parental reactions wrought by divorce can cause anxiety and insecurity. A baby manifests anxiety by crying, clinging, and being irritable.

### Recommendations

Stress can be caused by any kind of change. As much as possible, provide consistency and nurturance to your infant. Avoid angry and emotional outbursts in front of the baby. If you have daycare providers, try to maintain consistency with them also. Given the reality of divorce, there are often two working parents with similar work schedules which leaves only evenings and mornings to be with the baby. Dividing this time between two parents is difficult, but important for the child. A tremendous amount of psychological bonding between you and your child takes place during these early years. The nurturing opportunities abound for an infant, and this is where he learns to feel loved and cared for by both parents. If you and your baby bond closely during the first year or two of life, the chances increase that you will remain invested in your child's well-being for the rest of your life. The dependency that an infant exhibits sets the stage for you to take care of this vulnerable little person, who is an extension of yourself. The sense of responsibility that emerges for the parent during this time is great. Allowed to flourish, this same sense of responsibility and commitment will continue and your child will benefit.

Granted, there will be stress to the baby as he adjusts to two homes instead of one. But when your commitment to the well-being of the baby is there, the infant will feel it. Rocking and holding the baby while singing gentle lullabies will soothe anxiety and increase trust.

## *"Mine!"*

### *Age 1 to 3*

### *Description*

In this stage, a child's whole world revolves around him. He is struggling to be independent, and he is trying to figure out where the boundaries are. Much of a child's activity at this stage revolves around testing limits. The child needs freedom but also fences.

### *Divorce Anxiety*

Fears are often heightened because the child feels that his world is different from what he knew. The toddler may also have increased fear of separation, clinginess, and asking for the absent parent.

## Recommendations

A toddler needs order and routine. He needs an environment that is safe and predictable, with clearly defined limits. This helps him feel secure. A nurturing bedtime routine may help decrease his anxiety and nightmares.

# "I Have an Idea"

### Age 3 to 5

## Description

This is a time to try things out. A child plays very earnestly and watches grown-ups closely to see what they are like and what they do. Expect lots of questions from the child during this stage. She's trying to make sense out of the world she lives in.

## Divorce Anxiety

A child might feel that a divorce is her fault, "because I was bad." She may doubt her own lovability, "because I'm not good enough." Fearing abandonment and rejection, she may be overly compliant to parental wishes. If there is a lack of interaction between your child and one of the parents, the child will believe it's because of something she did. The preschooler may have difficulty adjusting to transitions between parents.

## Recommendations

Avoid expressions of anger. Very specifically provide clear and concrete explanations of changes. Explain to your child that she will be cared for, and reassure her that she is loved by both parents. Provide lots of opportunities for the child to express her feelings and fears through words and play. Play "house" with your child using dolls and props to recreate your own family situation. Allow the child to play the role of parent. This will give you a glimpse into how they view you or the other parent. This can sometimes be an eye-opening experience and a good time to re-evaluate how your child perceives your interactions. Give the child nurturance and affection during this stage, and teach her to speak up and ask for what she needs and wants. Be supportive when she does this. A child will need to hear she is loved more often during the divorce transition.

## "I Am Important, I Count, and I Can Do It"

### Age 6 to 12

### Description

A child wants to become good at what he is doing. His accomplishments give him a sense that he is really somebody, that he counts, and that he is no longer a child. He understands more about life now because of his increased intellectual capacity and emerging sense of morality.

My best teacher is remembering when I was six and couldn't understand why people fought and countries had wars.

### Divorce Anxiety

A child sees things in black and white: Someone is always right, and someone is always wrong. He reacts to the divorce by crying, withdrawing, feeling deprived and angry, and acting aggressively. He may have difficulty playing and feeling joyful. He may be unable to concentrate on school work because he is preoccupied with the divorce.

The child is beginning to empathize, and he worries about both parents' well-being. He feels ashamed of his parents' break-up. At this age, a child will have difficulty explaining the divorce to others. He will typically feel unsettled about it within himself, but he doesn't have the words to express the situation because it's not even clear to him. He may fluctuate, one day blaming Dad the next day Mom. As one eight-year-old put it, "My dad was messy around the house and this always bothered Mom. So she finally got mad enough about it and got a divorce so she wouldn't have to clean up after him." Another day he admitted, "My mom should have been more patient with my dad. He tried to keep things neat, but he was tired from working so hard so we could all have money."

This is how the child tries to make sense out of what is going on around him. If the explanations he's been given don't make sense to him, then he'll create his own, and they're usually black and white explanations.

Because a child usually wants to blame someone or some event he may feel the divorce is his fault. It's difficult for him to think in abstract form and understand the many complexities involved in relationships.

### Recommendations

Assure your child that Mom and Dad will continue to take care of him, and that he will continue to see both parents. Let the child know he has your permission to love the other parent. Encourage positive communication and contact with the other parent. Say positive things about the other parent. Listen to the child's feelings without judging. Help him express his sad feelings. Do not pressure him to take sides. Avoid arguing in front of the child.

# "I Am Who I Am"

### Age 13 to 18

## Description

A teenager is overwhelmed with physical, social, and emotional changes. By making choices in these areas, she is forming her individual identity. It is important for teenagers to relate with others socially and to compare feelings. Long talks with friends are essential tools for finding meaning and purpose in life. The teen's primary focus changes from family to peer group. Though less involved with family, the teenager needs extra parental guidance to launch her into adulthood.

## Divorce Anxiety

Distressed parents who are having their own problems may be unable to provide the extra support and firm limits that a teenager needs. The teen may resent being asked to assume more responsibility around the home because those duties pull her away from her peers.

Difficulty concentrating in school, chronic fatigue, and physical complaints may surface. The teen may express her emotional distress by becoming distant and aloof from the family. She may feel depressed and struggle with self-esteem. She will grieve over the loss of family and childhood and wonder about commitment and relationships.

The light shines brightly in the heart of a child.

## Recommendations

Provide opportunities for your teenager to share feelings, concerns, and complaints. Discuss issues and situations honestly. Do not pressure the teen to choose sides. She is able to understand that there is more than one side to every story. Avoid relying on her for emotional support. Encourage healthy friendships with other kids her age. Arrange for frequent contact with the other parent and allow friends to visit both homes. Be sensitive and flexible with the challenge of scheduling time. Ask your teen for ideas on how to arrange time between both homes. Try to use her ideas.

## Inviting Your Teen to Communicate

Consider using this letter as a guide if it feels right for you. Some parents have left letters such as this on their teenager's pillows, giving them the chance to reflect on the message as they drift into sleep.

*Dear (Son or Daughter),*

*Because I care about you, I want to understand what you think and what you feel. Because you're important to me, I want to feel close to you.*

*So I'm letting you know that if you open up and share your thoughts and feelings with me, I will respect them. Feelings are neither right nor wrong; they just are. I will try hard to simply listen and not pass judgment. I'm simply asking you to share with me so I can better understand you and your world.*

*I'm asking for your permission to let me into your mind and heart. I promise to treat your sharing and honesty with respect. In turn, I'll be honest with you as I use good judgment about what level of sharing is in your best interest.*

*For example, I will answer your questions about the divorce, but I will not share private marital matters with you. If either of your parents did this, we could not help trying to persuade you to see things our way.*

*You were created from both of us. You deserve the right to know each of your parents from your own experience. You can love both of us. We don't want you to take sides.*

*We truly want the best for you and we're sorry for the pain our divorce has caused you.*

*You are loved very much.*

*I hope that we can share some discussion on this very soon.*

> *Love,*
> *(Your parent)*

# "I'm Discovering Me and the World"
## *Adult Children*
### *Age 19 and Older*

## *Description:*

The tasks before a young adult are many. In today's world they have so many options they sometimes have difficulty deciding what to do. Relationships, careers, starting a family, social circles, political issues, causes, spirituality, all enter into their menu of choices, all options to consider as they grow into themselves.

## *Divorce Anxiety*

An adult child who learns that his parents are getting divorced will inevitably feel mixed emotions. One of the strongest reactions will probably be "Why?" The adult child will have seen that maybe the marriage wasn't perfect, but if it survived after all these years, why can't it go on working? Why not just stay together? There is a certain comfort in knowing you have two parents in one home to fall back on no matter how unstable the world is. With a divorce, this foundation of security will no longer be available to a young adult.

*Relationships are the result of our human need to connect with others.*

The other strong reaction will center around their own attitudes concerning relationships. They may start to question trust in other persons. They might begin to ask themselves, "If you can't depend on the stability of a twenty-five year marriage, what can you depend on? Do people change that much? Will my spouse change and no longer want me? Will I be abandoned? Will I end up getting divorced? What can I do to prevent my marriage from ending up in divorce?"

Answers they may come up with might include: "I'm going to do the opposite of what my parents did. I'll find a partner who really needs me and will never leave me (creating the basis for a codependent relationship). I'll never get committed because I'll just end up getting hurt anyway. I can't trust what I see because everything changes. It's all my dad's fault. Why couldn't he have been more flexible, more faithful, etc.? My mom is being so selfish, I can't believe she hurt my father like this."

## Recommendations

Talk to them as adults, acknowledging that both parents contributed to the problems in the marriage. Casting blame on the other parent could alienate the child from that parent, or backfire on you for trying to persuade them to your side.

Discuss the reality and difficulty of long-term relationships, while providing hope for the future. Reflect with them on what might have helped the relationship stay together. Also reflect on the reality that sometimes two people grow in different directions and they grow apart. This is no one's fault; it just happens sometimes. Let them know that sometimes life throws curve balls and the important thing is how you react to them. Accepting the challenge of what comes your way brings growth.

Words build trust when they are congruent with actions.

If adult children have families of their own, the question of how the divorce will affect the grandchildren will come up. Ideally, the relationship with the grandchildren shouldn't change. Reassure them that both parents will still be active grandparents and that the love you have for the grandchildren will never change. Assure them that both parents will still attend the grandchildren's performances, baseball games, etc., and that you will minimize the stress on their children. Then work towards accomplishing this.

Balancing honesty about the truth of relationships and maintaining hope and optimism for their future relationships will be the real challenge as you strive to discuss your divorce with your adult children.

## Children at Risk

There is a wide range of typical reactions to divorce, but it is important for you to know when your child is having problems beyond what is normal. Being sensitive to your child's thoughts and feelings will help you to detect problems that may need professional intervention. Professional help is usually indicated when:

- A problem behavior becomes constant instead of periodic.
- You feel unable to cope with the situation.
- There is a dramatic change in the child's personality.
- Symptoms remain the same over time and there is no improvement.
- When your child's sense of despair deepens to a point where he loses hope for the future and shows no interest in connecting with others.

Kids worry. I try to figure out what is going on. I know that kids are scared and they're hurt and sad. Kids do bad in school because of all the worry. They can't concentrate on anything but the worry.

—Jarmal, age 12

## The Stages of Grief

During divorce, children experience changes in daily schedule, family structure, living arrangements, and plans for the future. They suffer loss of possessions, social status, and relationships with extended family or friends. The natural reaction to any loss is to grieve.

Dr. Elisabeth Kubler-Ross, internationally known for her studies of the grief process, has identified several distinct stages that both adults and children go through when they mourn a significant loss, such as divorce. It is important to understand that these stages are not instructions about how to grieve, but merely guidelines for understanding a natural emotional process when one has suffered a significant loss.

Grieving takes a great deal of emotional energy. Your child may feel anxious and tired much of the time. He may have less energy for day-to-day tasks, school activities, and peer relationships. It is important for you to understand the grieving process your child

Tears are the safety valve of the heart when pressure is laid on it.

—Albert Smith

is going through and give him the freedom and support he needs to complete it.

Grieving is an individual process. Everyone progresses through its stages differently, and stages may be skipped or revisited at any time. Try to view the grieving process as an opportunity to get to know your child better. Does he retreat within himself, or is he a walking panorama of emotions? Regardless of how your child is reacting, he needs your support and care. When the grief is worked through, the lasting sadness will be manageable.

The insight that you gain from observing your child's style of coping will inevitably help you to connect with him during difficult times in the future. You might make a reflective comment to him about what you have noticed, such as "You know, Sam, I've noticed that you tend to get quiet and seem to think a lot when there are big changes going on."

Let your child know that what he is feeling is appropriate. You might say, "I want you to know that I respect how you choose to deal with changes, and I won't ask you lots of questions, because I don't want to bug you. But I do care about what you're feeling, and whenever you want to talk about it, you can count on me to listen, because I care a lot about what you feel and think."

Difficult times often provide the opportunity for hearts to reach out to each other. If you've ever had the experience of caring for someone who is ill, you may have noticed the vulnerable emotions that surfaced during that time. The same vulnerability occurs during a divorce, creating the opportunity for bonding that can more firmly cement a relationship.

When your marriage breaks up, it is not just your child who mourns. You are mourning, too. Your challenge is trying to function well enough to take care of yourself and your child, and, at the same time, work through your own grief process.

# Stages of Grief

## Shock and Denial

"This divorce isn't really happening." In this stage children will think thoughts that will help them deny the experience. They will lie about the divorce and tell themselves that this is just another fight, but everything will be back to normal soon.

## Anger

"How dare Mom and Dad do this to me!" Children will feel generalized rage at the world for allowing something like this to happen. They will feel isolated and furious that this is happening to them. They'll think it's unfair and may feel betrayed by one or both parents. Outbursts of anger in unrelated situations can occur.

## Bargaining

"I'll get them back together." Children under the age of twelve typically think that somehow they caused their parents' divorce and thus it's their responsibility to get them back together. Behaviors supporting this type of thinking includes over-compliance, scheming to arrange "get-togethers" for their parents, misbehaving to get the attention of both their parents, forging love notes from one parent to the other.

## Depression

"My heart feels broken." In this stage, absorbed in the intense pain they feel from having their world come apart, they can be overwhelmed with feelings of helplessness and sadness. They can start crying for no other reason except that they feel sad and need to release the pain.

## Acceptance

"My parents are divorced, but I still have a mom and a dad." Hesitantly at first, children begin to talk more openly and freely about the loss of a two-parent home. Their energy gradually returns and they pursue neglected interests. Their ongoing adjustment and acceptance will be affected by factors such as: parental conflict, flexibility in the schedule, ongoing contact with both parents, and freedom to deal with their emotions as they arise.

## Mirroring Honesty to Your Child

Remember that actions speak louder than words. Your child observes the ways parents conduct themselves and learns from their example. Good or bad, he most often imitates what he sees you do.

Johnny, age six, heard his mother talking to a friend on the phone. She had been crying just five minutes earlier, and Johnny had concluded that she was feeling sad about the divorce. However, she said to her friend, "I'm just fine; everything is going great."

From his mother's behavior Johnny was learning not to honestly express his feelings of sadness. His mother was teaching him to cover up his real feelings—to put on a happy face, even when he's not happy.

*The wisdom for the world lies in the simplicity of a child's heart.*

Without pouring out her feelings to her friend at that moment, Johnny's mother could have acknowledged the truth by simply stating, "I'm feeling sad about the divorce, but I'm starting to feel a little better, and I do know that things will improve." She might even have added, "But let's talk about something else. I've had my cry for today," if she really prefers to close the topic. If not, she might have added, "Sometimes it helps me to talk to a friend and cry."

In either case, actions and words should have been consistent. Her honesty would also teach the child not to hold his feelings inside.

Some children never learn to express their feelings. Instead they keep them bottled up inside. This is called repression. Pretending not to hurt is an unhealthy way to cope with unpleasant situations. Your child needs to feel free to honestly express his emotions. This is how both adults and children come to accept the situation and eventually resolve it. In fact, you may need to encourage your child to express his true feelings, especially during a divorce. All family members need to mourn the loss of the family as they knew it. Both parents and children must grieve as a part of the healing process.

## Brainwashing, Programming, and Alienating Your Children

During a divorce you may be tempted to sway the children toward your position. But doing that could cause them to feel alienated from the other parent. Wooing the children to your side during custody, time-sharing, property, and support conflicts can seem like a key to winning, but it is not fair to put your children in this position. Parents who do so are often motivated by their own feelings of rejection, hostility, loneliness, anxiety, or revenge. Whatever the reasoning behind such actions, however, they are inappropriate and ultimately destructive. Brainwashing, programming, and alienating children can cause serious, long-term harm.

In a recent study, *Children Held Hostage: Dealing with Programmed and Brainwashed Children* (Clawar and Rivlin, American Bar Association, 1991), only 140 out of 700 families (one out of five) showed no evidence of programming and brainwashing. According to the study, parents in conflict over custody and property, commonly program and brainwash their children more than once a day. Programming and brainwashing occur more than once a week in 50 percent of families, and at least occasionally in 80 percent. It is therefore reasonable to assume that some form of programming, brainwashing, or alienation occurs in most divorcing families.

According to the *Children Held Hostage* study, brainwashing is defined as "the selection and application of particular techniques, procedures, and methods" to implement a specific idea. It can be done directly or indirectly, and sometimes is so subtle that neither the child nor the parent is aware that it is going on.

> If she hadn't cut Dad all the time, it would have helped. I am part of my dad. I would have trusted a lot earlier. I loved Mom but didn't trust her.
> —Jason, age 18

If a father says to a child, "I hate your mother. She deserves to never see her children again," this is a direct attempt to program the child. On the other hand, if he simply fails to ask the child any questions about her visit with her mother, the programming is indirect and subtle, but still very powerful.

Programming is defined as "giving directions based on a specific or general belief system to a child, in order to obtain a desired end or goal."

Programming is taking place when one parent insinuates that the other parent doesn't care as much about the child because *they* didn't take them shopping for new school clothes.

Programming and brainwashing may occur over a long period of time, until the child responds with the behavior the parent is trying to create. Some children realize what is going on and even actively participate. Others, totally unaware, are unknowing victims.

All brainwashing techniques provide a damaging role model for children. Whenever a child is led to believe things that are not consistent with his perceived reality, he begins to question much more than just that circumstance. The Clawar and Rivlin study concluded that "brainwashing in the form of withdrawal of love causes great emotional damage." Parents must consider the potential long-term damage that they expose their child to when they engage in such behavior.

Brainwashing or programming can cause the following problems:

- Because the parent tells him that what he sees or hears or feels is not true, he begins to doubt his own judgment and perception.

- The child says untrue things in order to please one parent, only to feel guilty for lying and hurting the other parent. The child feels caught in a no-win situation: no matter what he does, one parent is disappointed. Caught up in the parent's battle, the child assumes responsibility for it and feels guilty.

> Parents can work together, maybe rent a duplex or something and live right by each other, so the kids could go with their dad and then with the mom. Kids need to be loved by both parents, not just by one. Kids get really depressed and stuff if they can't see both their parents. Kids should talk to their parents a lot and parents should talk to their kids, too.
>
> —Sam, age 8

- The child learns that it is okay to lie to achieve a desired outcome.

- If the brainwashing involves false charges of sexual abuse, the child may feel anxious and ambivalent about sexual issues. The memory associated with raising such sensitive issues will likely be retained and will interfere with the child's development of healthy sexual attitudes later in life. Lessons children learn about sexual matters affect their sexual attitudes when they became adults.

- The child may learn to be a pleaser, censoring her own feelings according to what is acceptable. She may develop very good antennae for detecting what is acceptable and become adept at feeling out the situation before deciding how to respond. Over time, the child becomes less able to identify her own feelings because she has become more in tune with others' emotions than with her own. As an adult, she may neglect her own needs and assume the role of pleaser, making only her partner happy.

- The child who is asked by one parent to spy on the other is a victim of conflicting loyalties. Regardless of how he handles the situation, he feels guilty for letting down one of the parents. The result can be depression, a feeling of shame, and increased distance from both parents.

- As the child gets older, she understands that she is a product of both parents. Hearing bad things about one parent may cause her to feel bad about herself. She reasons that if one parent is faulty, then the half of her that is like that parent is also faulty. Positive self-esteem is created in part from a healthy relationship with *both* parents.

- When a child discovers that he has been the object of programming, there may be a backlash against the manipulative parent. The child's love may turn to anger against the programmer.

I wish my parents would learn how to talk nice to each other, even if they are getting divorced. I'm sick of all the mean things they say.
—Todd, age 15

I grew up having my mother's eyes, my mother's laugh, my mother's words and my mother's anger for my father.
—Scott, age 17

According to the Clawar and Rivlin study, women are often the worst offenders. Bitter mothers represent the majority of likely programmers. The study contends that women have a sense of ownership of their children and a conditioned view of their role. Also, mothers are overwhelmingly "awarded" custody of their children and thus spend more time with their children.

As a parent, whether a father or mother, you should try to step back from time to time and take a look at the messages you are sending your child. All children need to have a healthy and nurturing relationship with *each* of their parents whenever possible. Remember that once upon a time you, too, could see the good in the child's other parent. Your child now stands at that point.

## Methods of Programming and Brainwashing

Trying to enlist the child to see things your way comes naturally during divorce—so naturally, in fact, that you may not be fully aware of what you're doing. You are programming or brainwashing your child if you engage in any of the following activities:

1. Denying the existence of the other parent.
   - Never talking about the other parent.
   - Not allowing photos of the other parent in the child's room.
   - Not relaying messages to the child from the other parent.

It bugs me when my mom asks me about Dad's girlfriend. I know my mom doesn't want me to like her because she's jealous, so I lie and tell my mom she's mean. But I feel bad about it. She's really a nice person. I feel torn because I care about all of them.

—Kim, age 13

- Blatantly ignoring the other parent at social functions.
- Refusing to acknowledge good times with the other parent.
- Making the child feel guilty for talking about the other parent.

2. Attacking the other parent's character and lifestyle.
   - Criticizing the other parent's family.
   - Attacking the other parent's career, or steering the child away from that career.
   - Remarking that the other parent is living in a relationship outside of marriage and is therefore an immoral person.
   - Refusing to allow interaction with the other parent.
   - Attacking the other parent's choice of friends or new spouse.

3. Placing the child in the middle.
   - Speaking to the child about issues that should be discussed privately with the other parent, such as visitation schedules, money matters, and child support.

4. Manipulating circumstances.
   - Not informing the other parent of school performances, sporting events, and recitals.
   - Embarrassing the other parent when she/he attends educational, religious, or social functions.
   - Listing a stepparent at school as the parent of record.

5. Exaggerating differences.
   - Instigating an argument with the other parent in front of the child, later telling the child that you were just trying to have a nice conversation.
   - Snickering or making faces in reaction to the comments of the other parent.
   - Taking minor issues and blowing them out of proportion in front of the child.

6. Making the child serve as an ally.

> If I come home from a visit with my dad and I'm really happy and stuff, my mom acts sad, like I have to be mad at him. He's still my dad, and I love him.
>
> —Sandy, age 10

- Involving the child in adult issues and asking for his sympathy and support. Saying things such as, "Do you think your father should have all the money?" Or, "Now that I'm sick, do you want to be with your father instead of me?" Or, "Your mother is taking me to the cleaners!" Or even, "If you were the mother, what would you do?"

- Making the child feel that the other parent is not sincere. Saying, "If she really meant what she said, she would . . ."

- Creating an image in the child's mind that you will be left poor and homeless if she doesn't stay with you. Saying things such as, "If I didn't have you, I don't know what I'd do."

- Telling the child that your life has been stolen by the other parent, and you won't let him/her steal the child, too. Saying, "He got the house and car, he's not getting you, too."

7. Threatening to withdraw love.

- Making the child feel that if she loves one parent, she will lose the other.

- Phoning the child at the other parent's house asking him if he misses you and wants to come "home."

- Encouraging the child to disobey the other parent.

- Threatening the child with punishment unless she tells you everything that happened during a visit with the other parent.

8. Rewriting reality for the child.

- Telling the child that the way the other parent cares for him is inappropriate.

- Creating events to demonstrate that the other parent is either inadequate, unworthy, or inferior.

- Telling the child she is wrong when she makes positive comments about the other parent.

A five-year-old made the following statement during therapy:

> *You are a bad mommy, huh? Everybody hates you, Mommy. It hurts my feelings when they talk bad about you, Mommy. Daddy*

We end all of our phone calls with "I love you." In a hurry, I forgot. She called back to ask, "Why?"

*can't see me happy with you, Mommy. It makes him sad. Duck so Daddy won't see you. He can't see me happy with you. Daddy hates you a lot. You don't pay him any money for me, huh? I love you, Mommy. Why does my whole family hate you? I have to tell the bad things about you, Mommy. Daddy told me to say those things so I won't have to see you anymore.*

## How to Prevent Programming and Brainwashing

Divorce is painful, but *you* can choose how to react to it, and the choices you make will have a profound effect on your child.

The chart on the page 45 shows some typical destructive reactions and the corresponding supportive reactions you can choose instead of the destructive reaction.

## What Kids Say about Brainwashing

Quoted from an interview with Amanda, a 17-year-old honor student:

*Well, brainwashing is kinda like this. While they are talking, I just sit there and say, "Uh huh, I understand." And then all of a sudden I find myself being persuaded toward the parent who is talking! I'm thinking, "Yeah, Dad was like that, or Mom does do that. Yeah, you are right." And then all of a sudden, my admiration and respect turns toward the parent that I'm with. But I will be with the other parent and I will start being persuaded toward what that one is saying. After a while I had to ask, "What am I doing to myself, and what are my parents doing to me?"*

*During that time I would have appreciated it so much more if they hadn't talked about each other—even if it meant that they didn't really talk about their own emotions to me. I could barely handle what I was going through myself. I didn't want to be their moral support. I didn't want to say, "Well Dad, it's okay, let me be this big moral support for you," because I could hardly handle what I was feeling myself. And the things that he would tell me would just make me hurt more.*

I just wanted to go play baseball with Dad and watch games and be more in touch, but anytime I said that, Mom would get real sad and then she would ask if I wanted to go off and live with him. I just wanted to get to know him. She started saying how horrible he was. He thinks that I think bad things about him, because of all the things that Mom says about him. I don't think he's bad, and I understand that Mom is just mad at him.
—Ryan, age 11

They always talked behind each other's back. So I didn't know who was right. I loved my dad and I wanted him to be the good guy because I wanted a good dad, because he had always been a good dad. But, then my mom would talk about my dad and Dad about Mom and I wondered how right they were really.
—Shane, age 17

*And so, maybe if the parents could focus more on the positive: "Okay, what do we do now? What is the next step? Let's not be sad over what has happened. Let's not talk over the past because all that it does is bring up hurt feelings and the whole situation." If you try to focus on other things and not always talk about the divorce, that's what makes you get over it faster.*

*I admire my parents. When I think of them, I think, "You are my heroes because you have turned a bad situation around." Keeping family together is very important. And it is good to talk about things. I don't mean parents should stop talking to their kids, but stop talking to the kids about each other.*

## One Last Comment about Manipulating Your Children

Your children need to be protected from manipulation, whether it is physical or emotional. It is not fair for one parent to manipulate the children in order to hurt their relationship with the other parent. This seems obvious to an outsider looking in. But if you are caught up in the intense pain that comes from ending a marital relationship, it can be difficult *not* to use such methods against the person who has inflicted pain on you.

As a parent, you must stop and consider the effect of the messages you send to your children. At the end of the day, think about the conversations you have had with your child. Were your messages supportive of the child's relationship with the other parent? Did your messages carry an undertone that warns the child against feeling at peace with both parents? Only *you* know for sure the intent of the messages you've been sending.

Here is an excerpt from a letter that one father wrote to his former wife after the children abruptly refused to have anything to do with him. The complete letter can be found in Chapter 5.

*Why are you stopping the girls from seeing me? Why are you poisoning their hearts and minds against me? I am their daddy!! Why can't you leave your personal feelings out of it and allow me and my girls a normal relationship? What have you told them to make them turn and hate me as much as you do—and so abruptly? I deserve to at least know what you have told them. Is your hatred for me so great that it has blinded you to the fact that by pulling the girls into it, you have caused them to have problems in their own family and have to have ongoing therapy when they are adults?*

I miss my dad when I'm with my mom, and I miss my mom when I'm with my dad.
                    —Lindsay, age 7

As a parent, you are responsible for creating an environment that is supportive of your child's right to love both parents. It is possible to reach a place where you can let go of the past, learn to respect the other parent, and build new and healthy relationships with your children and others. Through increased awareness and reflection, you can make the right choices and not fall into painful and destructive reactions.

Divorce is an opportunity for you to model tolerance and forgiveness to your child. Children are aware that parents can hurt them without meaning to; they, too, can learn to forgive.

| *Destructive Reaction* | *Supportive Reaction* |
|---|---|
| Custody of my child gives me exclusive rights. I decide what to do about school, medical and dental care, extracurricular and religious activities, and so on. My ex-spouse should have thought about being more involved before divorcing. | A divorce is intended to separate a husband and wife, not a parent and child. Each parent shares the responsibility for the child, even after divorce. I will inform my ex-spouse about what's going on in our child's life. I will consult with him/her about decisions concerning our child, in the same way I would consult with a business partner. |
| I love my child more than anybody else, including my former spouse. It's only natural that my child loves me the most. | I recognize that children are capable of giving and receiving love with many people. I see it as a healthy situation when others love my child, and my child returns that love. Love is not finite. |
| I'll get revenge on my ex-spouse for what she/he has done to me! I raised the child while she/he was out creating a new life. She/he doesn't deserve my cooperation and understanding now. | I have grieved over many things in the past. I've learned that holding onto bitterness will hurt me, as well as my child. I will continue to work on forgiveness. |
| How much money am I going to lose or gain? | I realize that divorce creates financial difficulties. I'll do my part for our children. |
| I want my ex-spouse out of my life. If I ignore him/her as much as possible, she/he will just go away and leave our child and me alone. I'll force restrictions on my ex-spouse's contact with our child. If that doesn't work, I will make my ex-spouse as miserable as I can! | Even though I ache inside over my marriage and divorce, our child needs frequent and continuing contact with both my ex-spouse and me. I will be respectful and acknowledge the good in my ex-spouse so our child can identify with the good in each of her parents. These actions build on the reality that our child was created by both of us and is part of each of us. |

## Children and Conflict

Divorce and conflict seem to go hand in hand. Most of us would prefer to avoid conflict, if given the choice, but it is important to remember that without conflict there can be no resolution. Conflict itself is not necessarily destructive, but how you handle conflict might be.

Throughout this book you will see the term "parental conflict." One of the most important things you need to understand is that there is a direct correlation between high parental conflict and the difficulty children have adjusting to divorce. All of the research indicates that it is parental conflict not the divorce itself that causes long-term harm to the child.

When children observe their parents in conflict over matters relating specifically to them (such as time sharing or child support), they tend to assume some responsibility for the conflict. When the conflict is centered on them, it is easy for children to believe they are the cause of it.

We know that children need parental approval. It feels good for them to make their parents happy. Child custody battles in which one parent is often the "winner" and one the "loser" can leave children feeling sad and somehow responsible. They often assume guilt for the outcome, and the burden can be too much to bear.

A certain amount of conflict is inevitable during divorce. But your responsibility as a parent is to try to keep the child out of it. It is the parents who are getting a divorce, not the child. Try to form a parenting partnership that is dedicated to the well-being of your child. Your child needs a good, strong relationship with each parent, both during the divorce and afterwards.

The courts and attorneys expect to see conflict between divorcing parties. Certain legal issues may remain in dispute for a

It felt like they were fighting because of you and not because of them. It felt like you were the problem and that you did it and you made it happen.

—Megan, age 9

long period of time before the court makes its final decision, although mediation and other options can decrease this time significantly. It is difficult but not impossible to separate disputes between you and your spouse from the family life you each have with your child. In the same way that you leave work at the office, you can leave your legal conflicts in the courtroom.

# 4

# *Repairing the Damage*

Divorce is an extremely challenging and frightening experience for adults and it is not possible to shield children from all the emotional fallout of severe marital conflict. So, realistically we need to recognize how easy it is to spontaneously react to the pain and say unkind things about the former spouse to the children. Nevertheless, these messages are inappropriate and when we let them slip out we inevitably cause children distress.

## *Conflict*

My former husband, Giff, and I thought we had successfully created a co-parenting relationship because we still communicated often, he stayed at my home with our daughter whenever I was out of town (staying at his home would have been difficult with her school schedule), we went to parent-teacher conferences together, and so on. But the reality between our intentions and our behaviors showed up in my daughter's face one day and left an imprint on me that I will never forget.

All three of us had been invited to a college graduation party honoring a special young man named Patrick who was a paraplegic. Giff and I had actually met because we were both involved in teaching Patrick to downhill ski, using adaptive ski equipment. We both loved Patrick and wanted to share in the joy of his success. We decided to go as a family.

We set out with good intentions. We were in my car; Giff was driving and Aimee was in the back seat. Within minutes, I noticed

> When I heard them fighting a lot and blaming each other, I would get mad, and I would say it was both of their faults, and they would just look at me. Then I would figure that it was now my fault that they were divorced.
> —Maria, age 13

that Giff was going the wrong way. There was a much shorter route and we were running late, so I offered advice. He quickly informed me that he also knew how to get there. Shortly thereafter, it was obvious that he was flooring the gas pedal of my Subaru, trying to get it to go up the canyon faster. I suggested that he try shifting gears. But *he* knew how to drive. It was as if we were still married.

At that moment, I turned around and looked at Aimee. She was sitting still with the skin between her eyebrows scrunched up. I saw her burden at that moment. The two people that she loved so much were arguing over directions and driving. How important were directions and driving and "being right" compared to her stress at seeing her parents in conflict? It hit me, loud and clear—I simply had to make peace with Giff, not artificial, but true peace. We couldn't fake it because she would know. The greatest gift I could give her would be my heartfelt peace with her father. She would feel it and her eyebrows could relax.

We went to the party and celebrated Patrick's accomplishment, but later that night I called Giff and shared my experience. Because I "owned" some of the responsibility for keeping the stress between us going, he agreed with me that we needed to do something. We had to break old patterns and think before we spoke or acted.

We decided to see each other in the special way Aimee saw each of us. We knew that was in love, but certainly not a romantic love. We could find a new way to love each other and from there we began. As ideal as it sounds, we agreed to that and made a commitment to each other. So far, so good. The following poem expresses my feelings about that night.

The most important thing is to realize that kids are affected— emotionally, academically, and socially. I can tell when there is something wrong, even if they don't tell me. They become withdrawn or depressed or aggressive, but it comes out.

—Nancy
6th Grade Teacher

*We shared in faith*
*And trusted one another*

*In oneness we connected*
*Our hearts*
*Our bodies*
*Our secrets*
*Our souls*

*All blending*
*To create yet another life*
*A life beyond either of us*

*A life with its*
*Own heart*
*Own body*
*Own secrets*
*Own soul*

*We can't possess a life*
*We merely participate in creating it*
*This life needs its roots*
*To know its legacy*
*This life needs to be cherished*
*To know love*
*This life needs wings*
*So it can soar alone*

*But first*
*This life needs you and me*
*to be at peace*

## Self-Esteem

Self-esteem is the measure of a person's perceived inner value. Positive self-esteem comes from receiving positive feedback from one's environment and from oneself through positive self-talk. Children with high self-esteem feel secure about themselves and their immediate world. They are confident about the future and do not worry about instability in their lives.

Divorce is an unsettling experience that creates feelings of insecurity. Children do not know what to expect and often worry about the future. Their sense of security is threatened.

High parental conflict has been proven to have an adverse

A flicker of hope
That life can still smile
When I'm in deep despair
And feel beyond repair.

Still I muster the strength
And go deeper still.
My child needs me now,
To heal our hearts some-how.

effect on children's self-esteem. Children base their identity on the perception they have of their parents. Their sense of self is derived from both mother and father. If children continually hear about the faults of their parents, they may begin to see those same faults as part of themselves.

A study of college students who had experienced divorce as children concluded that divorce alone does not cause a reduction in self-esteem, but that *the higher the conflict between the parents, the lower the young adult's self-esteem.* The preservation of a child's healthy self-esteem in a divorce situation is clearly dependent on how the parents choose to act.

As a parent, make a concerted effort to help your child adjust to the many changes taking place in his life by providing comfort and stability. As your family life begins to stabilize and it seems that things will work out, the child's sense of security will return and self-esteem will improve.

As you think about the conflict that has occurred during your divorce, ask yourself the following questions:

- Have my children been exposed to parental debates and loud arguments?

- If so, how did they react?

- How did they feel to hear arguing? Did they take sides?

- How can I protect my children from conflict in the future?

- What type of apology do my children need from me, if any?

You can make decisions that protect and enhance your child's self-esteem. Parental actions that promote self-esteem in children include the following:

- **Reassure** your child that he is loved by both parents. Talk to your child about the unconditional love you have for him. He needs to hear you express it.

- **Listen** to your child without judgment. You are letting him know that his thoughts, feelings, and values are important and valid.

- **Provide specific and meaningful praise** when your child engages in an activity. Don't offer blanket praise; be supportive but honest. Your child will learn that you mean what you say.

- **Share** meaningful activities with your child. Look for opportunities to start a conversation.

- **Be consistent** in setting and enforcing limits. Knowing the limits makes a child feel secure.

- **Make it clear that the divorce is not your child's fault**, especially during the initial phases of divorce. Explain that "Mom and Dad are divorcing each other, but neither of us is divorcing you. We both love you and we always will."

- **Be responsible and respectful.** Your child will imitate what he sees you do.

- **Help your child set realistic, achievable goals.** Share in his excitement and pride when she reaches them.
- **Deal with anger in healthy ways.** Be a role model of appropriate ways to deal with anger.

## Damage Control and Repair

### *What if I have already done things that hurt my child during the divorce?*

It would be wonderful if negative comments could be avoided entirely, but that is simply not reality. Remember that 80 percent of all children who experience their parents' divorce report that at least one parent has talked negatively about the other. Everyone makes mistakes and slips up now and then. The important thing is what you do after you realize your mistake.

Children who have been negatively influenced against a parent need to spend significant time with that parent in order to receive and process new firsthand information. The relationship between a child and a parent can redevelop in a healthy way if nothing is done to sabotage the effort. Often, grandparents and relatives can help support your child to undo the "negative talk" by sharing information that helps the child see the good in the parent.

A stepparent can be a positive influence in a child's life, but not at the expense of the biological parent. Whenever possible, the child needs the personal security of a healthy relationship with her original parents. Do not try to replace a parent with a stepparent. The stepparent should be an add-on, not an "instead of." Give the child plenty of time to establish and maintain a healthy relationship with each parent.

Some parents underestimate the effect that arguing has on a child. To understand what parental fighting does to a child, remember that when a fight occurs, the child feels compelled to take sides. In the child's mind, whenever there is a fight one side must be right and the other wrong. The child makes this assumption independently and is left to draw his own conclusions.

If your child has overheard you and your ex-spouse fighting

I just wanted to say that you need to be careful when you are getting divorced, not to be so mean. Do it slowly because my sister got really messed up and she started going through all kinds of changes. And it got me depressed. Parents should tell the kids all about it and help them understand.

—Andy, age 11

over child support or visitation, it becomes a mutual responsibility to apologize to him. Your child deserves to have both his parents admit they've made a mistake and are sorry for the pain they've caused him.

*My child's heritage is hers alone. I cannot wish it away. She knows she is made up of both of us, good or bad and I must respect that.*

### Some open disagreement is to be expected, isn't it? After all, we are divorced.

Do not underestimate the significance of ongoing disagreement to a child. Not long ago, I was in a sixth grade class filming a video, sitting in a circle with twenty-eight students, discussing divorce. About half the children had experienced divorce. I asked, "How many of you have heard your parents arguing?" All of the hands went up without a second thought. The next question was, "How many of you felt sad when you heard your parents fight?" Every single hand went up again.

What those children were saying is that it hurts to hear two people they love arguing with each other. Many of them felt a real need to share their painful experiences and have their feelings validated. As they acknowledged each other and shared experiences, a solid sense of honesty and trust developed in the group.

When you as a parent make mistakes, an apology goes a long way toward creating a relationship of respect, trust, and honesty with your child. Children have feelings that need to be validated. When parents apologize, they create space for a closer bond to develop.

The turning point of one of the more painful divorce cases I worked with was an apology made by one of the parents to the children. The children had been exposed to ongoing disputes and had developed an extreme loyalty to their mother. This caused them to turn against their father and refuse to see him. They blamed him for starting fights and causing the divorce.

In the father's mind, the children's perception of him was distorted. He had been trying to correct that perception but had not been well received. The children became even more entrenched in their position.

I told the father to assume that what the children were thinking was totally true (which indeed it was for them). "If their thoughts were totally true," I asked, "how do you think they would be feeling? What might they need from you in order to get over those feelings?"

The father drafted a page of comments to each child, written specifically to address what was troubling each of them. He wrote some of the most validating and reassuring comments I have ever seen a parent make to a child. After I shared these thoughts and feelings with the children their hearts were softened.

A high degree of conflict between parents during and after the divorce process is associated with many types of adjustment difficulties in children.

Children need validation for their feelings and recognition of what they've gone through. When this happens, there is respect. When there is respect, there is honesty. And with honesty comes trust. In a trusting environment, children will share their feelings, and the pain they are holding onto will be released.

## *What do I say when the other parent has a serious problem?*

Many parents struggle with what to say to a child when she has actually witnessed problem behaviors in a parent. Knowing that the child bases a part of her identity on each of her parents, what should you tell her about a parent who has had drug or alcohol difficulties, problems with the law, or other serious problems?

- **Be direct**. Do not whitewash or minimize. The child knows the truth when she hears it. For example, "You know that your mother has some problems in her life. She has a disease called alcoholism, which means that she drinks too much alcohol, and that affects the choices she makes in her life. I know that you wish she would spend more time with you, but her drinking gets in the way of her doing that. She has made choices in her life that have caused these problems."

- **Let the child know he does not have to "identify" with the parent** by making the same poor choices that the parent made. He can identify with the "good parts" that have been obscured by poor choices. This is an important distinction to make, because children have a natural tendency to imitate their parents.

You might say, "Underneath the poor choices your mom has made, there is a good person inside, and that is the person you came from. Every person has a good side. Sometimes it's hard to see because of her poor choices, but it's in there somewhere. We just have to look harder to see it. You don't have to make the same choices she has made in her life. You can make choices that make you feel happier in life and won't cause you the same kinds of problems that she has."

Let the power of forgiveness heal the pain of yesterday.

- **Encourage the child to brainstorm the things he likes** about the other parent, and assist him with this if he gets stuck. Sometimes it may feel like a real stretch for you to note any positive characteristics, but it is crucial for a child to see some good in each parent.

You might suggest to the child, "Why don't we think of the good things about your mother that you have seen over the years? She has a pretty smile, and she is kind to animals. She likes to be funny and make people laugh. She makes really good chocolate chip cookies. She reads stories, and she can sing well, too."

- **Help your child to notice how many of the parent's admirable traits she also has**. This will deliberately align the child with the positive aspects of that parent. When she identifies with the parent, she will have positive traits to focus on rather than negative ones.
- **Reminisce with the child about good times** with the other parent, whether the child was present or not. Doing this

supports some of your reasoning for getting married and gives evidence of the good person inside both parents.

## How do I apologize? How much honesty is too much?

As a rule, consider the age of the child and what he can handle. Do not overburden him with adult issues that may only confuse him and cause him to worry. I have listened to some young children provide detailed accounts of one parent's extramarital affairs. This is obviously inappropriate information for a child to have. Such matters are obviously better left to the adults. As children mature and begin to notice things on their own, you will have the opportunity to help them explore their thoughts and process what can be learned from their experiences.

I'll always remember the day my six-year-old daughter came home from first grade and announced to me that she couldn't trust me anymore. Taken aback, I asked her why. Apparently, at school that day, a child had been caught telling lies to the other children. The teacher took the opportunity to discuss the importance of telling the truth and that lying creates a lack of trust. When I asked my daughter what she thought I had lied about, she said I had lied when I told her that the world was very large, and that it would take weeks to travel around it. We had been looking at a globe as we discussed this.

Later, I had bumped into an old friend in the grocery store and made the comment, "It's a small world!" When my daughter overheard that comment, she thought I was contradicting what I had previously told her. It made me smile to think about the weighty issues that can trouble six-year-olds, and it was one more opportunity to mull over life's little lessons.

I recently had another experience that reminded me of just how honest young children can be. While waiting in line to board a plane, an energetic girl announced to everyone, "Today is my birthday! I'm five years old!"

A spirited but noticeably overweight man behind me invited the singing of "Happy Birthday" to one very pleased little girl. She zoomed in on the friendly man and said, "My mom would love you!" The curious man asked, "Why would your mom love me?" The little girl confidently answered, "Because you like to eat and she likes to feed people. I never eat enough for her, but you look like you eat plenty!"

People in line weren't sure what to do. . . silence. Then the man said, "You're right! I do eat too much and it's not good for me. The world needs more honest people like you. Have a wonderful birthday!" The girl quickly perked up again and said, "When you're not so fat you can run faster like me," and she proceeded to show him how fast she could run.

The honesty of a young heart hits home again.

My child looks me in the eyes and I see her confusion.

What am I telling her in all of my mixed messages?

I must remember humility and admit my mistakes and teach that goodness lies deep in each and every heart.

When you feel like hope is gone, just ask for some love! ♡
and you will get it!

Truth is not complex. Just ask a child.

# 5

# Open Your Heart and Communicate

The ability to listen and communicate is a gift that some people seem to be born with. Being able to explain yourself and understand others is one of the most important abilities that a person can have. People in all types of careers work hard to develop their communication skills.

Spending your time and energy to learn how to listen and communicate well is one of the most wonderful gifts you could ever give to your child. Clear communication can create a strong, lasting bond between the two of you.

Imagine that your child has had an experience with a bully at school. He feels humiliated and embarrassed by it. He holds in his feelings of pain until he gets home. Then he wants to talk with you about it and looks for an opening to do so; however, you are busy getting ready for a PTA meeting. While continuing to work on your report for the meeting you ask him how his day was. He doesn't feel that you truly want to listen to what happened to him. He shrugs, "It was okay." You ask him if he wants a snack.

Your child's state of vulnerability won't allow him to open up and talk about his sensitive experience unless he detects support. It is too painful to risk talking about something traumatic unless there is some guarantee he will be supported, so he doesn't say anything.

A few days pass, and there have been few opportunities for meaningful discussion, so he puts off telling you and tries not to think about it. But the pain of the event is still there. It is simply repressed. The child has pushed his emotions deep down inside.

Repression of emotions eventually leads to high frustration, depression, even poor health. He needs to express his feelings in order to get through them. Healing begins by discussing feelings with someone the child trusts and getting the reassurance and comfort he needs.

Parents are not mind readers and can't always tell when a child needs to be listened to. Children often look for openings to talk about their feelings and experiences; but before they open up, they need to feel a sense of security and support.

My pedestal should be short enough that my child can climb on top.

Try to create an environment where the child knows that if she needs private, individual attention, you will be there for her. If you consistently demonstrate your willingness to listen, you will create a healthy and open environment.

This is a letter a five-year-old dictated to her mother shortly after her father moved out of the family home. She was longing for her father and wanted to "identify" with him, and therefore hoped he would also get an ear infection, just like her.

> Dear Dad,
>    I got an ear infection today. Maybe you'll get one like me. Jessica got one, too, and her mom took her to the doctor.
>    Someday I want you to live with us, but I know you don't want to.
> > From,
> > Samantha Wilson
> P.S. Please write a letter to me, too.

Another letter, also dictated by Samantha to her mother, exhibited other common feelings of this age group when a parent leaves home. Young children often wonder if the parent left them because the parent didn't like/love them.

*Dear Dad,*

*I love you. I want to see you soon.*
*And I really love you because I like everything you do and I'm trying really hard to make you like me.*
*Do you know you love me? I want you to come to my mommy's wedding.*

*From,*
*Samantha Wilson*

Samantha also felt that problems between the mother and father stemmed from his being overweight. Sometimes when Samantha used to watch him eat, she would feel angry at him because she didn't want him to be fat. She thought her father could see inside her head, and since he knew what she was thinking he must have left her because of that.

When she states, "I really love you because I like everything you do," she is trying to make amends in hopes her dad will come back.

As parents, we need to be more responsive and listen to all children who hide their quiet pain and shed their tears alone. Over a million children a year in our country are being affected by divorce. These children need attention. If their own parents are hurting too much to listen, the rest of us must try to be attentive. Children everywhere are carrying burdens of pain, and they need our compassion and understanding.

Good listening can be learned and developed over time. We can *all* make a difference, but we need to start sometime. Let it be today.

Through my years of work with children of divorce I have been impressed by the touching message that most children expressed of wanting both their mom and dad to remain in their lives. Their desire and need to feel connected to the two people who brought them into this world moved me to write the following song lyrics. This song represents what I believe most children of divorce want to say to their parents.

*When you told me the news*
*I quickly knew I stood to lose*
*My family as I knew it*
*Would no longer exist*
*My sadness feels so great*
*But it's worse with words of hate*
*It doesn't have to be so bad*
*A few kind words would make me glad*
*When I hear your words of scorn*
*Inside I feel so torn*
*I don't want to have to choose*
*Because then I really lose*
*So please respect me when I ask*
*Not to put my interests last*
*Even though right now we're all in pain*
*It's peace we have to work to gain*
*Parents are forever*
*And forever never ends*
*It's time for all*
*Our hearts to mend.*

## How to Listen

- Pay attention. Notice when your child needs to talk. Take the time to give 100 percent attention to your child.

- Make eye contact with your child when you ask questions.

- Use reflective listening skills. Acknowledge the child's statement by repeating what you believe he said. Try: "It sounds as if you are worried about trying out for the team because you think you might not make it."

- Be specific when you ask questions. Ask: "How do you think you did on your spelling test today? Did it help to do all the practice tests last night?"

- Don't forget to give physical affection when the child needs comforting. Children of all ages need affection. Young children like to cuddle in a parent's lap, while older children appreciate a pat on the back or a hug.

- Schedule one-on-one time with each child as often as you can. This can even be time to do chores together. The point is that you are spending time with the child to listen to his concerns, his interests, and his joys.

## Listen for Feelings

Be alert to what your child may be feeling. Ask questions such as: "Is there anything worrying you right now?" or "How do you feel about . . . ?" Reassure her that she can share her feelings and worries with you. Show her that you care how she is feeling and want to help. Always honor her feelings by saying, "Feelings are not right or wrong, *they just are.* You are important to me, so it follows that your feelings are important to me also."

Realize that some of the feelings your child has may shock or surprise you. Never say, "You don't really feel like that," or "You shouldn't feel that way." The fact is that the child *does* feel that way, even if the reasoning leading to that feeling is faulty. Say instead, "I didn't know you felt like that." Then try to explain the confusion and misdirection.

Reflective listening mirrors the child's feelings in a supportive way. It also reassures the child that you are listening. By saying, "It sounds as if you feel angry. Is that right?" you are acknowledging that you received the message and understand. It's important to ask the child if your presumption is accurate in order to avoid presuming something the child may not have meant.

The following sections give examples of what you can say when the child expresses certain feelings.

### Uncertainty, loss of predictability, routine, and security

Acknowledge the changes. Talk openly about them. Emphasize what the child can rely on. Divorce brings many changes to a child's life. The child will adjust to the changes, but he may feel insecure as he moves through this transition period. With very young children, it is especially important to try making changes gradually.

> I would like them to tell me that they love me. I didn't care when they were together, but when they got divorced, they wouldn't say they loved me that much anymore. That was the time when I needed it. They should sit down and ask their kids how they are feeling and why. And tell them that they love them a lot and just don't forget to tell them you love them.
>
> —Missy, age 12

> Every baby is cradled with love and endearing words. As they grow, a child's need for affection doesn't stop and neither should our expressions.

## Rejection by the parent who left home

Both parents need to continually reassure the child that she is loved by both of them. Demonstrate this message with your actions. Arrive on time when meeting your child, and plan activities that provide a high quality of interaction. Show an interest in her daily activities by attending school functions and extracurricular activities. Make phone calls to her, and keep a photo album full of pictures of her.

> My mom just doesn't like us very much. First she left us and moved away, and now she won't give my dad money to help take care of us. I wish she liked us more.
> —Chris, age 8

## Helplessness, feeling out-of-control, and fear of the unknown

Acknowledge these fears, using reflective listening. One of the most important things a parent can do is express empathy. Children's feelings are important and valid. By demonstrating that you care about their feelings, you validate them.

## Choices in Communication

Take time to analyze your conversations with your child. Try having conversations solely for the purpose of gathering information. Don't try to change the child's perceptions. Just listen to the things he says. Tape conversations and listen to them later. Then you can analyze your reactions and determine where you might have been a better communicator.

> You feel like you want to run away, you don't want to be there. You want to say, I'm sorry, I didn't mean to do that. Don't yell anymore.
> —Trenton, age 13

Try to avoid using the following words and phrases, because they *prevent* effective communication:

- Threatening: "If you don't . . . "
- Commanding: "When I say jump . . . "
- Intimidating: "Because I said so . . . "
- Blaming: "Why don't you ever . . . "
- Preaching: "I've told you time and time again . . . "
- Correcting: "You should have done it this way . . . "
- Lecturing: "If I've told you once . . . "
- Putting down: "You don't know anything . . . "

## Actions Which Encourage and Support Effective Communication

- Look into your child's eyes.

- Sit down so you are at the child's eye level.

- Listen without interrupting.

- Restating: "It sounds as though you are feeling. . . "

- Empathizing: "I'm sorry you are in so much pain right now. Is there anything I can do to help?"

- Respect the Timing: "Maybe you don't feel like talking right now, but when you do, just let me know."

Yeah, I have heard the term *failed marriage.* If my parents failed, then I must have, too. It makes you feel weird, makes you think you are from a weird family.
—Steve, age 15

Responding to your child in a healthy way also requires making a conscious choice to be supportive rather than destructive. Choose words that promote healing.

| Win-Lose Words | Family-Friendly Words |
|---|---|
| Single parent | Co-parent |
| I have custody. You get visitation. | Shared parenting |
| Visit your mother Visit your father | Spend time at mom's house Spend time at dad's house |
| Visitation schedule | Time-sharing plan |
| This is all your mom's/dad's fault. | You don't have to take sides; you can love both parents. |
| Failed marriage, broken home | You still have a family, even though your parents live in two different houses. There is nothing wrong with you. You are not "broken," neither have you "failed." |

Communicating a message to someone through a song, poem, or letter shows that you cared enough to take the time to create something special for the situation. This is a song I wrote to Aimee about her parents' divorce. Children like songs, poems, and cards. I deliberately made the choice to represent both my feelings and her father's because I wanted to reinforce that she is loved by both of us. When it comes to love, it's not an either or option. Children need love from both their parents. Be sure that you take advantage of appropriate opportunities to reassure your children of their other parent's love for them, as well as your own.

### May Your Heart Be Filled with Trust

*We wish that we didn't have to say*
*That things are going to be this way.*
*Your mom and dad will be living apart,*
*We're sorry to bring any pain to your heart.*

*We both want to have you as part of our life...*
*We'll try not to argue or cause further strife.*
*Our divorce didn't happen because of you,*
*There really was nothing at all you could do.*

*We went different ways, but now we both agree,*
*We'll be the good parents you need us to be.*
*We'll be working together to show you we care,*
*Whenever you need us, we'll try to be there.*

*I know you're hurt by the changes we're all going through,*
*Please trust in a future that's kinder and new.*
*Your father and your mother are still here to stay,*
*And the love we both have for you won't go away.*

## Your Children and Their Friends

As your children get older, many of their personal concerns are related to their peer relationships. This is a natural and normal part of childhood development. Children need to learn how

to venture out into the world and develop their own individual relationships with people beyond their family unit.

For a child to inform his friends that his parents are divorcing can pose a dilemma. It is confusing enough for him to understand his parents' divorce himself, and most often, the explanations he hears or assumes to be true do not make total sense. Given this situation, how can he possibly try and explain the changes to his friends? It is a true challenge and one that parents should be aware of so they can offer the necessary help when wanted (or needed).

Ask your child if she wants help in explaining the divorce to her friends. If she does, consider having a surprise party at your home and inviting her friends. This idea comes from a real situation: a child in our neighborhood whose parents were divorcing was having a difficult time. She was feeling abandoned by the parent who left the home, had assumed that the divorce was her fault, and was now assuming that her friends didn't like her anymore. Seeing all of this, I organized a party for her. We called it our "Because You're Special Party." We had balloons, streamers, cakes, games, and fun. All of the kids wrote notes to Leslie telling her how much they liked her. The friends were very sweet. It's amazing to me how empathetic other children can be when the need for compassion is pointed out to them. Needless to say, Leslie glowed from all the attention. The party also gave her a chance to talk to her friends about the divorce with some adult guidance.

## Advice from a Teen

The following is an interview with Amanda, a seventeen-year-old honor student. She reflects on her family's struggle to communicate during and after divorce.

E. Hickey: It sounds like you paid a lot of attention to your parents' feelings. Did you get your parents to listen to what you were going through? Were you able to tell them about your pain?

Amanda: Well, at the time, I was living with Mom. I would have appreciated it more if she would have listened to what I was saying. I know it was a very difficult time for my mom. I understand now more than I did then. I would have appreciated it if she could have been more sensitive to how I felt. Whenever I couldn't handle it and would cry or say, "Mom, I don't like what you are doing," she would become defensive and uptight and say, "I wish you wouldn't act that way," and just be on the edge. I know that it was hard for her because she had so many other things to worry about, but parents could be more sensitive. That really could have helped; and I really wish at the time that I could have turned to her. Since I couldn't go to her and tell her how I was feeling, I went to my best friend. If I hadn't had my friend, I don't know what would have happened to me. It's good for the parent to be that best friend, because not all kids have a friend that they can turn to.

I felt like no one supported each other in the whole family. Everyone was just doing their own thing, and they only cared about what they were doing. Maybe if we would have gotten together and talked more, and maybe if we would have supported each other more in what we were doing—at least know what each other was doing—maybe it would've worked out better. I felt completely on my own. I spent a lot of time with my friends, but as far as the family unit went, I felt like it was collapsing. I was pretty mature, but not all kids are. A lot of kids, once they think their family has stopped caring, start getting into things like drugs.

E. Hickey: You said something really important. When kids feel fragmented and distant from their family, they lose that sense of support and reach out for drugs. What other things might a teenager do if she's not feeling support from her family?

Amanda: Maybe she'd start with serious relationships. She will cling to her friends—regardless of who they are. If she's the type that's into dangerous things, it might stop her from taking school seriously and make her lose focus on what is important in her life. If I don't have my family, then nothing is really important. Kids can lose their sense of where they are going and what they are shooting for.

E. Hickey: If a parent truly wanted to connect with a child, what could she/he do?

Amanda: Some parents have that desire to understand and to be sensitive to what their child is feeling. But they are so caught up in what they're feeling and what they're going through that they probably can't handle hearing what the child has to say. So they become defensive. I know it must be difficult to try to put themselves on the level of the kids and say, "OK, I'll try to do this better. I'll try to understand." Most parents really do care, whether the child knows it or not. They just can't show it. But if they did, that would help a lot.

E. Hickey: So you agree with the idea that parents need to invite their kids to express their emotions?

Amanda: Yeah, they need to initiate it. I guess the kids could; but if they get a negative response, then they are going to back off.

E. Hickey: And they won't share their feelings?

Amanda: Right.

E. Hickey: Can you tell me more about sharing feelings?

Amanda: The parent needs to be the one to go to the child and say, "How are you feeling?" and be sincere when they say it. When they are being totally sincere, then the child will open up. The child realizes, "My mother or father will hear what I have to say now, and they are going to listen." If the parent can always put themselves in that position and be there for the child, they will be more responsive. It all depends on the parent's attitude, whether the child keeps their feelings in or not.

E. Hickey: Is it the nonverbal things that keep the child all closed up?

Amanda: Well, you know when a parent is being sincere. You know when parents really want to know what you have to say. I mean, I can think of times when my parents were like, "Oh, well, tell me what you . . ." and I could tell that they were just saying it because they were obligated to. I could also tell the times when they really did want to know what I was feeling.

E. Hickey: How would you have felt if your parents had created an environment where they said to you, "OK, I care about what you're going through. I know this is hurting for you. Please tell me about your feelings. Your feelings are neither right nor wrong, and I won't get mad at anything you say, but just please tell me about your feelings. I really want to know."

Amanda: I think that would have been great. I would be much more open, and I would feel much more relaxed talking with my parents if they said something like that.

E. Hickey: So what you're saying is that parents need to invite their children to express their emotions about what they're going through.

Amanda: Yeah, they should tell them that they are not going to get upset if they say something that they don't like.

E. Hickey: So you would have felt a lot better if one or both of your parents had sat down and said, "Tell me what's going on with you." You would have started opening up?

Amanda: Yeah, I would talk to them about things that were on my mind. Even now, after the divorce, I don't really like to go up and talk to them. I feel like I'm going to get a negative response, so I keep it to myself.

E. Hickey: Should parents give out ground rules? Say something like, "Whatever you say is fine. I'm not going to get mad at you if you tell me something that you don't like about me or my behavior." Do they have to come right out and say that?

Amanda: That would have been amazing if they would have said that! I really admire a parent who could say that. If they are willing, it will really help communication.

E. Hickey: It is then a learning experience. The parent can learn how the child feels and adjust to it.

Amanda: Right. I mean, no kid will dare to criticize their parent unless they are sure the parent can handle it. If the parent really wants to know, they will get a response. Then they can work with that, and they can learn from what the child has to say. The child will feel better, because they will have honestly shared what they feel.

E. Hickey:  So your message to parents would be: Keep a sense of family. Keep the communication open so that kids don't feel lost out there on their own, because if they flounder, they may reach for things that aren't healthy.

Amanda:  Right. If there is always fighting and tension and no one can hardly stand to be around home, then the family starts to collapse. When you are with your kids, try to be in the best mood possible. Understand, be sensitive, care, and show that you care. Open doors to communication, and let the kids know that they can come to you and tell you how they feel.

You can choose to be a good listener for your child. It may take some work and practice, but it is a worthy goal; listening is a wonderful gift.

# 6
# Security and Reassurance

Can someone reach
Inside my pain
And let me know
Things will be okay again?

One of the most frightening feelings children have during divorce is uncertainty. They are unable to control lives that once felt fairly stable, and they are unable to make decisions that will affect their future. This chapter offers two strategies for alleviating a child's feelings of fear and insecurity.

## Reassurance

During my divorce, my daughter and I talked a lot about what was going on. Often she would raise the same concerns over and over and listen to my reassurances again and again in an effort to feel secure. When so much seems to be crumbling, mere repetition can be reassuring. Of course not all children are talkers. Some children clam up and don't want to talk; they act out their fears instead, adding to the general stress and emotional chaos. Exert your best efforts to be patient. Hear beneath the questioning and negative behavior. Hear the truth of the plea, "Tell me again that we're going to be all right. Show me that I matter." After listening to my daughter's questions and concerns, I wrote her the following letter. Perhaps your own adaptation of this letter could help you explain things to your child.

I have to do something to make this better. What if I can't do anything to get my parents' problems settled? What if they leave me?

—Leslie, age 9

*Dear Aimee,*

*I know it's hard for you to have your mom and dad apart. Big changes like this can be scary. You might even feel all mixed up inside. I'm sorry that the divorce has caused you pain. I just have to tell you some things, and I hope you will listen.*

*Parents don't get divorced from each other easily. We thought a lot about this before we made the choice to get a divorce. Maybe one of us didn't even want to get a divorce, but sometimes when a choice is made by another person, we just have to go along with it. Sometimes we can't change other people's minds. We both knew it would be hard for you, but our problems with each other were big enough that it was too hard for us to live together anymore. We didn't want to have arguments and feel unhappy. Living apart from each other will help us, in time, to feel happier and more peaceful. And if we are happier and more peaceful, we will be happier people to be around.*

*We won't be happy right away, because it takes time to get there. Even though we made the choice to get a divorce, it still makes us both sad inside, just like it probably makes you sad. It's OK to feel sad and mad—that's normal. Most families who have a divorce between the parents feel sad about it for a long time.*

*But many of these families start feeling better about things after time helps them get used to the big changes. One of the big changes for children is having two homes—their mom's house and their dad's house. After spending time at both houses, you will start feeling comfortable at both places.*

*Aimee, some of the things children learn after their parents' divorce that you may want to think about are:*

- *The divorce wasn't their fault. It didn't happen because they did something wrong, because they weren't good enough, because they fought with their brothers and sisters, because their report card wasn't as good as it could have been, because they got mad at someone, or because of anything they did at all.*

- *The parents got a divorce because of problems between the two of them. It had nothing to do with the children. This makes children feel better because many of them have spent a lot of time worrying about what they did to make the parents get a divorce. They have also spent a lot of time trying to think of ways to make their parents get back together again. Once they learn that they didn't do anything to make their parents get a divorce, they realize that there is nothing they can do to get them back together again. When they understand this, they quit worrying about adult things and are able to think about kid things again, like their friends, games, school, and birthdays.*

*Aimee, do you know that we are getting a divorce because of us and not because of you? We are getting a divorce because your dad and mom cannot live happily together anymore. But we both still love you, and we always will.*

*It might be hard for us to show our happy feelings during these sad days, but that doesn't mean we love you any less. We love you more than any words can possibly show. And we both hope that you love us even more than that huge heart on top of the Empire State Building!*

*Love,*

*Mom and Dad*

## More Reassurance

Divorce is a passage in your child's life when you need to find as many ways and occasions as you can to say, "I love you." Love is no longer something your daughter or son is taking for granted.

Don't be afraid to be silly and expansive in your expressions of love to your child. When it comes to showing your love, the more the better. Here is an excerpt from a children's book my daughter and I wrote together. Perhaps it will give you some ideas.

### I Love You More Than Words Can Tell

I love you more than I could fit in our house,
I love you more than a monster mouse.

I love you more than the biggest snowflake,
I love you more than the best birthday cake.

I love you more than the brownest mud pie,
I love you more than the biggest blue sky.

I love you more than my favorite teacher,
I love you more than a fairy creature.

I love you more than a huge apple tree,
I love you more than a Band-Aid on my knee.

I love you more than all the aunts,
I love you more than twenty pairs of pants.

I love you more than my fly-fishing pole,
I love you more than the biggest dirt hole.

I love you more than a soft teddy bear,
I love you more than a cozy rocking chair.

I love you more than the hilliest mountain,
I love you more than a chocolate fountain.

I love you more than the most graceful ballerina,
I love you more than a laughing hyena.

I love you more than you could ever know,
Even more than a million words could show.

## Creating a Sense of Security: Two Houses, Two Homes, Two Calendars

To help alleviate some of the frightening feelings and increase your child's sense of security try to help your child feel as comfortable as possible in both homes. Surround her with familiar things. Keep everyday items available at both houses so the child doesn't have to be concerned about forgetting things. Here is a suggested list of supplies to help your child feel welcome in her second home:

*Love is not finite; Love is infinite.*

- Age-appropriate toys or games, including puzzles, crayons, markers, paper, books, balls, stuffed animals, dolls, and sports equipment.

- Clothing, including underwear, socks, shoes, clothes, pajamas, and outfits for special occasions.

- Food, including fruits, vegetables, staples, easy-to-prepare meals, spaghetti, tacos, and soups. Also include emotional boosters like popcorn, snacks, and ice cream.

- Pet supplies, if necessary.

- Photos of *all* family members.

- Boxes or dressers for keeping the child's things.

- Toiletries, including toothbrush, hair care items, deodorant, and other personal hygiene supplies.

- A calendar showing when the child will be at each home.

You can put some sense of control back into your child's life by allowing him to make small decisions whenever possible. Allow him to choose his own clothing or the restaurant when you are eating out. These decisions are not major or life-changing, but will make a difference to the child who feels that his life is out of control.

## The Calendar Concept

Keep the child informed about every aspect of his life. To demonstrate to children that you are in agreement concerning time sharing, it is recommended that both parents keep identical calendars visible indicating which days the child will spend at which home throughout the month. To begin the "calendar concept" for young children, color code the square for Mom's days with her favorite color, and use Dad's favorite color on his days. A dotted line can be used for shared days.

Both parents should agree to implement a daily routine of looking at the calendar with the child, and checking off the day that has passed, and noting when a change to the other parent's house will occur. Young children do not understand the concept of time, and will find it reassuring to "see" when they will be with each parent.

For older children, place a "D" on the calendar for days the child will be with Dad, and an "M" on the days the child will spend with Mom. Both you and your children will appreciate the quick reference while making plans throughout the month.

## For the Long-Distance Parent

Divorce is hard enough under any circumstances, but it is of special concern when one parent must move out of state. The child not only loses the parent from the home, but must also cope with having him/her at a great physical distance. Here are some practical ideas for bridging the gap between parent and child over long distances.

- Send letters, notes, and postcards often. Give the child a stack of stamped, self-addressed envelopes and ask him to write you back. One child sent her father an envelope full of New England color—some fall leaves. It was a "wish you could be here" message that he'll never forget.

There is a miracle
In every new beginning.
—Herman Hesse

- Write a story for your child. Give the main character in the story the same name as the child. Make it an affectionate and bonding story that shows her how much you care for her.

- Record favorite songs. Sing songs that the child loves, or that you have enjoyed together in the past. Remember that your voice is an expression of you, even if it isn't opera quality, and that's what counts to your child.

- Record a message. Hearing your voice does more for your child than a hastily written letter.

- Videotape yourself reading bedtime stories. Your child can play this at bedtime and enjoy the closeness of your almost being there.

- Videotape your new surroundings. Your child needs to feel that he is still part of your life. Showing him your home and the sights around your new city will help to keep him close to you.

- Exchange photographs. Let the child know that you're interested in what she's doing, too. Prominently display the photographs you receive.

- Give the child a memento of you—something simple such as a tie pin or some earrings. The child will remember you each time he looks at the memento. Being entrusted with something that is special to you will make him feel important.

# 7
# Caring for the Caregiver: Adults Grieving

When you told me you were leaving,
I knew then that I'd be grieving.
Knowing that we'd be apart,
Created a loneliness within my heart.

All my dreams included you.
How can I begin to make it through?
The pain of memories long past,
Hurt worse because we didn't last.

Everywhere I seem to turn
I'm being faced with things to learn.
No matter where I walk,
Your shadow seems to stalk.

When I think of how things used to be,
The hurt just overwhelms me.
But now it's time for me to heal,
Move on and find what else is real.

As the days turn into weeks,
And the weeks flow into months,
The memory of your face fades
And I can make it through my days.

But then you wander back into my life,
And I question if I'm all right.
I think its best to talk on the phone,
While I learn to stand alone.

When I'm strong enough again,
I'll let you come and be my friend.
But until I get the message to my heart,
We'll have to stay apart.

Parenting is demanding. To be fully supportive of your children when you are under stress and in a major life transition is difficult. For your sake and for theirs, *you need to take care of you.*

As you travel through the challenging phases of divorce, you need to know that your feelings and thoughts are normal and that although it won't be easy, there is a light at the end of the tunnel.

As a therapist, I am concerned that people who are in the process of divorcing take care of themselves. The following suggestions may help you do so.

## 1. Feel the pain. (Realize, then release it.)

The ways in which marriages end vary greatly. However almost all marital endings have one thing in common—feelings of disappointment, anger, and resentment toward the person who did not fulfill your dreams.

Denial causes you to bury those feelings temporarily. But unless the pain is felt, it cannot be released. Denying your feelings can be compared to getting a sliver under your skin. You can cover it, ignore it, or pretend that it doesn't bother you. The reality is that the sliver hurts and the longer you let it stay bedded inside you, the more of an irritant it becomes. After a time, it can become a festering sore. Unacknowledged frustration and anger over your divorce will fester and infect your attitude in other unrelated situations.

Parenting is challenging enough without the added turbulence of buried feelings. It is important to acknowledge your pain.

> The heart has its reasons that reason knows nothing of.
> —Blaise Pascal

## 2. Allow Yourself to Grieve the Losses Associated with Divorce.

Outlined in Chapter Three are the five stages of grief that most people go through when suffering a significant loss. Divorce involves loss for everyone. Become familiar with the stages as a reminder that your emotions and thoughts are not abnormal, but are, in fact, healthy and normal. Even cycling back in the progression is to be expected. As one of my clients observed, "I noticed that it was possible to go through the entire process in one day, and then start over again the next day. I would start out each morning in 'denial,' the first stage, and by the end of the day, I would have reached 'acceptance' again."

To review these stages, I include entries from my journal which illustrate the different phases of feeling and thought.

Letting go of control
And allowing the
Unfolding
Will permit the healing

## Stage One: Denial

This is only a mid-life crisis. He's going to come to his senses soon. I just need to be supportive and allow him freedom to go through this phase. After all, this is outlined in books. It's a predictable life stage! Give him space.

## Stage Two: Anger

How could he be so cruel? I have been patient and supportive, only to be rejected. He doesn't deserve to be happy after what he did to me. And I will make sure he is never happy again.

## Stage Three: Bargaining

Okay, maybe I haven't been compromising enough or attentive to his interests and needs. He always wanted more companionship and I was always so busy with my projects. I'll take up fly-fishing and plan some romantic times together. That will get things back on track.

## Stage Four: Sadness/Depression

I called to tell him I had made some special plans for us. He is not interested. "I'm sorry. It's too late," he says. I feel so sad, so alone.

### Stage Five: Acceptance

It hasn't been easy, but I do understand that things were not great between us for a long time. He seems more at peace with himself now, and my heart still loves his heart. He's a good person and I want him to be happy.

I can't make him feel happy with me. I don't want him to be with me unless he means it. And the truth is, he doesn't mean it. He might stay for Aimee's sake, but where does that leave me? Not secure . . .

At this point I feel a sense of relief that he initiated the changes that are going to move us both ahead. I have faith in the future, and I am actually excited to see what may be in store for me.

---

### *Knowing That Most Things Break*

*You fondle routine's*
    *tattered strings*
  *hugging dailiness*

    *blown*
*from room*
    *to room*

    *by dusty*
        *urgencies*

  *bent*
*against*

    *remembering.*

          *—Emma Lou Thayne*
         *in* As for Me and My House

---

## 3. Resist the Desire for Revenge

Going through a divorce floods you with some of the most intense emotions you may ever feel. The intensity of these emotions can cause you to react in ways that you never considered yourself capable of—and which you may later regret. During the times of greatest stress, you will find it difficult to sort out choices in your best interest for future happiness from those motivated by a strong natural impulse for revenge.

---

## The Ruin

The basement is black
    but in the noon hours the sun
    streaks in so you can see.
It's like coming upon a pile of bones.
The chairs are tipped on top of their table
    having dumped their occupants for dinner.
The forks are rolled in plastic
    having touched too many lips.
The blanket has been pulled from under
    the weight of those that were there
    and in its fold is the smell of you.
The cord is wrapped around the buttons of the phone
    hiding its face from my bulging eyes.
I know I cannot call.

It's like finding one of those ruins at Lake Powell
    where all life has been blown away.
Only this time I am the dead
    in this windless decimation.
My stomach is hollow
    and in the box of pictures
    all those teeth that show
    belong to skeletons.

—Megan Thayne Heath, 1983
in *As for Me and My House*

---

In the interest of healing hearts, talk to yourself about how you are feeling. The more you inventory your emotions, the clearer you become about your motives. It is much easier to make wise choices when you are clear about your feelings and motives.

At one point near the end of my marriage, I was filled with a strong rage at my husband. I had several almost irresistible opportunities to exact revenge and hurt him back. I understood the phrase "sweet revenge" as never before.

But I chose not to react. For one thing, I did not want to be known as a vengeful person. For another, I reminded myself that this person is the father of my child. If I hurt him, I also hurt my child because whatever pain he carries will be present when he is with her. For her sake, I could not hurt him. But it was not easy. I had to remind myself of who I was and how I wanted to be remembered.

Remind yourself of who you are when you are in a vulnerable emotional state. Take steps so you don't compromise your future and live with regrets.

### 4. Be Open to the Chance to Fly Solo Again.

Being in a marital relationship alters your identity, blending it with another's. Both partners make compromises and assume new personality characteristics to balance the relationship. When that melded identity is dissolved, you need time to rediscover who you are now as an unalloyed, independent self. Give yourself a chance to grow accustomed to the new you that is different from what you were *before* you married and what you were *within* the marriage.

Beware of dragging old baggage with you into a new relationship. Now is your chance to sort it out. Decide what interaction patterns or personality traits may have impacted your last relationship. Change the things you don't like, and avoid bouncing into a new relationship too soon. Above all, give yourself time to heal.

Equally important, treasure what's good about yourself. Now is the time to identify strengths and traits that perhaps were not valued by your partner. Possibly you love to ski, or read novels, or hike, or whatever, but always felt guilty because your partner considered that activity a waste of time and resources. What parts of yourself have remained dormant or self-censured for the sake of other goals? Let your next most important new relationship be with your Self.

Many social functions not only include couples but are also structured around couple activities. If you are not at ease in that

What brings two people
Together one day
May also be the same
Things
That separate them
Later

setting yet, don't accept well-intentioned invitations to couples' functions. Take time to become comfortable hanging out with yourself. Get back into enjoying your own company.

I gathered from my clients a few suggested ways to release pain, open doors, and establish a new center of balance.

- When your feelings are surfacing, write them down. Let them flow. If your feelings are conflicted, let the different parts of yourself argue it out with each other. Don't worry about being consistent. Don't worry about how you *should* feel. Find out what you do feel in all its contradictory richness. Scribble over each line or tear the paper to bits when you are finished. You want to release the feelings, not re-read and recycle them.

- Join a support group where you can talk freely about your feelings without feeling judged and without having the information get back to your children and ex-spouse.

- Scream into a pillow.

- Escape into the movies and the relief of caring how someone else's story will turn out.

- Sing songs matching your feelings. Read poetry.

- Attend sporting events.

- Learn to ask for what you need, and teach your children to do the same. Perhaps you need some time alone—or even time-out so you can calm down! Say so.

- Renew your connection with the earth—desert, lake, mountain, ocean, even a city park. Spend some time alone even if you go with friends.

- Apologize to your children about any pain you may feel you have caused them: "I'm sorry I've been so grouchy. It's not your fault."

- Practice deep and slow breathing. Use sighs and stretching to let go of stress.

- Daydream about being in your favorite place with your favorite people.

Go forth into the busy world and love it. Interest yourself in its life, mingle kindly with its joys and sorrows.
—Ralph Waldo Emerson

The heart holds the necessary power to heal itself, if it is willing.

- Commit to an exercise program tailored to your lifestyle and needs. Brisk walking is as good as a run. Being physically fit helps you feel and be emotionally resilient. A good workout also helps you let go of anger and anxiety. The point isn't to experience pain, but to feel your strength building.

- Make a list of all your interests and a wish list of things you would like to do. Prioritize and begin.

- Walk, swim, kick or throw a ball. Run, dance, jump on a trampoline. Go to bed sweaty and exhausted instead of teary and sleepless.

To these, let me add two from my own list.

- Renew your spirit. Whatever spirituality means to you, explore it more. We sometimes limit our spiritual growth by thinking about spirituality only in terms of our religious upbringing or church affiliation. These roots may still be strong and nourishing, but challenging times can be seasons of new growth. Seek your own personal connections to a higher power. Meditate, pray, listen, and connect. This can renew your faith in yourself when you most need it.

- Give of yourself to someone else. Although you may feel reluctant to connect with someone else's sorrow or difficult circumstances when you are hurting yourself, reaching out to others can provide healing benefits to you.

I'll always remember the Christmas after my mother died. The previous four years I had gladly spearheaded a "Sub for Santa" project at an agency for abused children. But that year I felt bowed down by my own grief and loss. I forced myself to go forward anyway, although at times I did my share of the work with a numbed and distracted heart.

My efforts were repaid in an unexpected way on Christmas Eve. Delivering gifts to children that night, some of them accidentally saw me. I saw their faces light up with delight and

> If life were predictable, it would cease to be life and be without flavor.
> —Eleanor Roosevelt

surprise, and my heart revived. Their youthful joy brought me back to the moment and to life. What we give to others will return to us in abundance.

## 5. Forgive

If your situation is such that you can cultivate kinder feelings, forgiveness is the most freeing option. Hatred binds us to its object as mercilessly as does love. Forgive and move on, or stay angry and remain stuck.

*In the depths of winter, I finally learned that within me there lay an invincible summer.*

*—Albert Camus*

As time went on, I realized that I still loved my former husband for the person he is. Even though I no longer want our marriage, I can appreciate his kindness, his love for nature, his sense of humor. He is a person with character flaws like the rest of us. I can focus on his goodness which will benefit my daughter, him, and myself; or I can focus on his faults, which will only hurt him, our daughter, and me. Harboring regret, bitterness, and anger at others or yourself catches you up in the double-stranded nets of guilt and blaming.

Start by forgiving yourself—for not seeing it coming, if nothing else. Then extend the circle as you can. You will regain your balance and forward momentum as you stop berating yourself for the past. Your new task is to be open to the future and the possibilities it holds for you.

My heart is usually
Kind and warm
But now it sings
A different song

This pain cannot stay
I look forward
To a brighter day

## 6. Own Your Pain

Every wounded heartache will continue to influence your life through the choices you make. In order to gain control over the choices you make and your reactionary behaviors, you must heal your heart. There are no shortcuts. One of the most important things you can do as you adjust to your divorce is to take responsibility for resolving your heartache.

We often see the heartache of wounded partners channeled into hurtful behaviors long after the divorce is legally settled.

Obviously their retaliation and revenge is sad to watch, yet these acts continue every day. If hearts were truly healed, the motivation to hurt and exact revenge would not be there. At times, these acts of retaliation are taken out not only on former partners, but also on other innocent persons who have become involved in current relationships with the ex-spouse.

Jealousy often ignites when the possibility exists that an ex-spouse is sharing private intimacies with a new person. At this point the pain really intensifies. As we look back, the very act of getting married implies the turning over of your most private self to another. This takes a great deal of trust. Simply by doing this, there is an unspoken trust communicated within this monogamous commitment that is simply understood and gradually becomes taken for granted. It is probably in this arena that a certain ownership or entitlement develops. Once a person becomes a spouse, their identity also becomes a part of your identity through the marital relationship. Consider the introductions we use: "This is my husband John." At a subconscious level, there is an assumption being made that your partner is now a part of you.

All of this is important because it often gets played out when the couple is trying to separate. In reality, we all know that we don't own another person, and never will. However, subconsciously the marital identity takes time to undo. For the years you were married, there was a joint identity as well as each of your own individual identities.

If the breakup of the marital identity has not had sufficient time to heal before a third person is introduced, the emotions and jealousies can be intense. Simply put, it can feel like another person is intruding on your turf without your permission and consent. These are the situations where we often hear about "crimes of passion" being committed. When a male or female

From a place of intimacy we move to formalities. Courtesies, and politeness now require strength.

feels like their "space" is being taken away by another person, especially when the person is still in love with the former spouse, the desire to put an end to the pain often results in hurting one or both of the participating parties.

The "reactionary emotions" to this type of situation can be prevented by recognizing inner emotions about your former partner and doing a lot of self-talk. The type of messages you need to be telling yourself during these times are expressed in the statements on the following page. Affirmations can help you recognize that you are a whole person regardless of the structure of your family.

# Healing Affirmations

Every person in this world has their own mind and freedom of choice. I cannot make another person want to be with me simply because I want to be with them. I recognize that I can't control the choices of my former spouse.

**********

I might be able to influence another person's perception but I can never control it, and trying to do so will make me so frustrated that I could end up doing things I will regret. It is in my best interest to let go, and release trying to control others, especially my former spouse.

**********

Although my spouse and I shared a certain "marital identity," I now have to release that identity and continue to progress with my own individual identity.

**********

I do not need to compare myself to another by wondering why a different person can please my former spouse. People change, and in doing so, their needs and desires change. This situation is not a statement about my self-worth or my ability to love and be loved. It is a reflection of the changes that have taken place over time.

**********

My children need my attention now. Becoming overly self-absorbed in my own pain can magnify and distort the situation. I choose to focus my energy and thoughts on things that I can influence and change, and not on things that are beyond my control.

**********

Although I may want to strike out and hurt the person who hurts me, it is not in my best interest or my children's best interest to do so. I recognize that putting out negative energy will return negative energy to me in some way. Therefore, I choose to send out positive energy even when I don't feel like it.

# 8
# Domestic Violence

Domestic violence is not justified or acceptable under any circumstances. It is a destructive and dehumanizing way to treat other human beings. For the onlookers, often the innocent children, acts of domestic violence clearly teach that conflict can be handled using acts of violence. If for no other reason than protecting the future of our children (yet there are many other pressing reasons), we must acknowledge the reality and brutality of domestic violence.

Acknowledging the reality also means understanding that domestic violence is something that both genders inflict upon one another. Violence towards any person, whether verbal or physical, is not acceptable and is always counterproductive if we want to teach our children healthy human values. We must put a cease fire on the war of gender issues. While we debate the rights of each gender, we are modeling to our children that the other gender cannot be trusted. Is that what we really mean to do?

Our concerns need to be focused on advancing well being, not setting it up for another debate. Eventually debates will exhaust the resources of our country. We must find a way to create peace among the genders, among the cultures, among the people, among family, but especially among parents who are the first teachers a child has.

Unfortunately, some families have a history of domestic violence. When an event happens over and over again, one learns to expect it. In time, it becomes a way of life, as does the coping strategy for such madness. When a marital relationship has been marked with recurring episodes of domestic violence it is extremely important to seek professional help, particularly when steps are taken to end the relationship. This is important because years of history and patterns that have been allowed to continue, create a false feeling of "normalcy" surrounding the abuse.

We have all seen how extreme the two sides of domestic violence can be. On the one hand, we see the appearance of love between two people, and then in their privacy, we learn that screaming, fighting, and hitting are a way of life for them. In order for a person to cope with the craziness of these two extremes, they learn how to justify and rationalize the events, such as "this must mean that he/she really loves me or they wouldn't act so passionately. I can tell how sorry she/he feels for doing this." Once a person is caught up in this cycle it is difficult to think clearly and make proper assessments of the situation. This is exactly why the help of a professional in the area of domestic violence may be essential.

The mere suggestion of "leaving the relationship" when domestic violence has slowly created an attitude of "ownership over the spouse" can spark such rage that the violence-prone spouse will become actively violent in frightening ways. Legal protective orders may help keep the raging partner at a distance, but when emotions and jealously flare, protective orders don't mean much to a person. Common sense is often lost in the heat of the moment. This is why crimes which are motivated by matters of the heart are called "crimes of passion." It is the passion of the heart that motivates the rage.

Many of these crimes are committed when the rejected spouse becomes aware that another romantic partner has been introduced into what was previously "their space." A person with a wounded heart interprets this as being "replaced" by another person. This situation inevitably aggravates existing problems. We should not underestimate the intensity of a person who feels rejected. To a person still in love with their spouse, the very thought that their lover no longer wants them, creates intense pain. Left unchecked, the pain of being rejected and feeling that their very core is not "good enough" can create madness.

A woman I worked with said that she wasn't afraid of her former husband hurting her because she would always have the kids around her and he would never hurt her in front of them. She thought this was logical. However, he did finally attack her in front of the children. In the heat of the moment, the consequences of his actions and words did not cross his mind. He simply reacted to the intense emotion he was feeling. Later on, he felt ashamed and regretful and had difficulty rebuilding the bond of trust with his children.

In divorces where domestic violence has been present throughout the marriage, it is illogical to assume that the person being divorced will suddenly act rationally and respectfully. Caution in terms of legal, physical, and emotional protection must be taken for the sake of your children and yourself. Support from knowledgeable professionals in the area of domestic violence is often needed so that hearts can be healed and patterns can change.

## Situational Domestic Violence

I must repeat again, **domestic violence is not justified or acceptable under any circumstances.** The very act of physically, mentally or emotionally hurting another human being, especially one that you love (or have loved) is wrong. At the very first indication that you might be capable of committing a harmful act, you need to seek help.

Letting go of something (such as the marital life) or someone you want, is very hard to do and your character will be put to the test. Having interviewed hundreds of parents during my years of child custody evaluations, I've discovered that there are many reasonable parents who have never had an episode of violence during their many years of marriage, until their "uncoupling process." It was during the separating process that many upstanding individuals temporarily lost their good judgment and said horrible things to each other, or hit each other.

One of the most common things I heard about was one or both parties throwing things, either at each other, or just throwing things into the air. Having heard enough of these stories, I concluded that throwing items must be an instinctive reaction for releasing anger.

I can't offer data on the frequency of these types of angry outbursts, but I can confirm that acts of abuse occur more often in the "uncoupling process" than we may want to admit. I think it is important that we don't lump these "reactive" situations into the same category with relationships that have a history of chronic domestic violence because they have very different etiology and require different therapeutic approaches.

If you understand the possibility for intense emotions to rise during the separation process, you can catch yourself before you may be tempted to sling harmful words or engage in violent physical acts. The roller coaster of emotions you will feel during your separation and "letting go process" is common in divorce.

What you do with these turbulent emotions is your choice. Pondering your options before the situations present themselves will help you follow through with appropriate actions. When you fail to consider these choices prior to arriving at vulnerable points in the process, you leave yourself open to reacting negatively, and even violently, to shock and pain. Anticipating emotional intensity and mentally setting boundaries beforehand will help you manage the difficult emotions you will be experiencing.

Below are guidelines for dealing with the pain you might feel when you're exposed to a deep romantic wound, such as seeing your former partner with a new romantic interest:

## Diffusing the Anger

1) Take a step back from the situation. Don't move into the situation any further, it will only cause more grief.

2) Tell yourself you are okay and that you just need to get some space away from the situation.

3) Remind yourself that this is not a statement about your self-worth. It is merely one person choosing another companion who may or may not be more compatible with them than you were.

4) Play over in your mind all the things that are important to you, such as your children, your character, the stability you have created in your life, your other family relationships, and so on. Remembering these significant aspects of your life can help protect you from caving into your desire to get revenge against the person who rejected you.

5) Talk to friends. Ask them to listen to you first without responding so that you can release the pain of what you have just experienced. After they have listened, then they can offer ideas and supportive suggestions.

6)   Continually use "self-talk" reminding yourself that these are stressful times, but they will eventually end and life will feel good again.

7)   Open your heart to the grief work necessary for letting go of a significant relationship so that you can truly heal the wounds your heart has suffered. Holding onto the pain keeps you "stuck" and will cause the pain to replay itself over and over again. Choosing the path of healing will free you up to make different and healthier choices in the future.

## Preventing Domestic Violence

Children in our country are being exposed to violence every day. They watch violence on television and in movies, witness fights at school and on the streets, hear their own parents arguing and yelling—and we wonder why there's so much violence in our society. We watch one group after another claiming that they have the "right" to be treated fairly and civilly in our country, all the while fighting violently amongst each other.

Who wants to be handled with violence? What are we role modeling for our children? If we are fed up with the violent approaches to conflict in our society, these questions need to be addressed. Teaching conflict resolution skills early in childhood, preferably in the schools where conflicts arise between peers, would allow for "hands on" opportunities for children to learn to resolve problems peacefully. Principles of mediation and problem-solving should be taught *throughout* a child's schooling.

The toll that inappropriate expressions of anger have taken on our society is severe. I recently heard two nine-year olds talking. One child said, "So what are you gonna do about it?" The other answered, "I'll have my dad beat him up. My dad is big." Is this the type of problem-solving message we want to be teaching our children? What takes place in the context of divorce creates an

> Your wounded heart was
> never healed
> And now your anguish
> is revealed
> Anger and pain can be
> so strong
> They blind you to what's
> right and wrong

opportunity for modeling healthy conflict resolution. Children need to learn "win-win" solutions as opposed to "I won, he lost." As parents, the choice is ours. What message will we teach?

My friend and colleague, Carroll Zahorksy, M.D., attended the **Conference on Human Rights** in Vienna, Austria in June 1993. Following are excerpts of a written statement he delivered at the conference. He discusses the importance of family in teaching accountability and responsibility in our world.

The family is where a child first sees or does not see respect for self and the rights of others. It is here that each child's sense of value is first perceived. In this place called family each child takes his or her first measure of what he or she is or is not worth. It is in the family where each child first measures the value of another. It is here where respect or disrespect for human rights is born. It is in the family where a child first sees two people sharing love or not doing so. It is in the family, first and foremost, where these values are expanded upon, developed, and embraced or rejected. **It is in the family where we learn to love or not love.**

Communities throughout the world are being damaged, even left in ruin because the heart . . . the family . . . and healthy 'family experiences' which instill respect for self and the rights of others are being devalued, sometimes decimated by principles of living and societal systems that are failing the people comprising them. Few communities are left unscathed. People are hurting everywhere. The family is again under fire. Societies are on trial.

The question is whether you recognize that there is a need for enhancing the good, changing the not so good, healing the hurting, sharing love, and respecting the rights of someone else.

The family is continually exposed to elements and influences that tend to erode its healthiness and devalue its worth. Conflicts arise and without healthy, effective methodologies for positively resolving conflicts, families are fractured and the health of a nation's people as a whole suffers. The incidence of violent crime in communities throughout the world is increasing directly proportional to the disruption and disconnection of families. The absence of fathers in the home is linked directly to this process. In the United States, it is estimated that as many as 80% of all individuals convicted of violent crimes grew up in homes having absentee fathers.

As a major step to these ends, I propose new and creative processes for dealing with family issues whether families be intact or in a state of separation or dissolution. I propose a Family Court System that removes families from the adversarial processes that are associated with most other processes and elements of civil law. This Family Court System would address matters of the family involving inter-personal relationships and matters of the heart. Every state could benefit from such a court system.

If something effective is not soon introduced into systems around the world to connect and reconnect families and create models and vehicles for stimulating greater value and sense of worth, the emotional and economical expenses and devaluing of the family will only get worse. The unhealthiness of societies will surely continue to escalate out of control. I believe people and families everywhere are inherently valu-able. I believe people want to find the good in themselves, others, and in the world in which they live. I believe people are willing to pay whatever price it takes to make the world a better place for their children, themselves, and others.

This requires the courage to chart new paths. It requires the maturity to preserve and effectively use that which is good and what works while being able to see what is not good, what does not work, and what is better turned loose of. In the expanding wholeness and healthiness of families, communities and civilizations can flourish and human rights can be honored universally.

# 9
# Keeping Your Balance: Separate but Connected

After practicing divorce mediation for years and completing well over 300 child custody evaluations, I have learned that every divorce story comes in two versions. Even two compatible people can experience exactly the same event and describe it very differently. The differences become even more dramatic between divorcing partners because divorce is such an intense, emotional experience.

Richard Gardner, a clinical professor of medicine at Columbia University, lectures extensively throughout the United States about divorce and custody. He notes that during custody litigation heightened emotion causes physiological changes which alter perceptions. When intense emotion is involved adrenaline is released to the brain, causing a person to experience what is happening at an accelerated rate. This acceleration during emotionally intense situations may distort the perception of what has occurred.

Even moderate feelings of pain, hurt, and loss affect how a person perceives a situation. When feelings are more extreme, they can affect a couple's perception of their past history together as well as the present. Divorce is one of the most painful life experiences, especially when children are involved, because parents feel that part of their own identities are being lost. To validate and justify their position, many parents spend a lot of time and energy trying to convert others to their perspective and to create allies.

During my evaluations I often hear two rational, educated adults describe the same event and give totally different accounts—both equally convincing in their arguments. Each account must have validity because, after all, each is a firsthand, eyewitness account of the events. Although I am concerned with sorting out whose version is most accurate, I also take into account the accelerated emotional state parents are in when going through divorce, because it can and does alter their ability to be objective. It's important that parents seek a stage in their healing where heightened emotions will not destroy their ability to make sound decisions.

It is difficult for parents to make decisions about the future of their children when they are feeling so shaken and vulnerable. Even after a divorce is final, many parents have a hard time moving past the hostile, negative post-divorce relationship because they have not divorced emotionally. The relationship continues to pre-occupy them and drain their energy.

The goal is to get past the emotions and make good decisions—get through the pain and get on with the growth. The first step is to get over the hurdle of emotions so that decisions are not purely reactive. To do this you must reach a stage in your healing where decisions are as carefully thought out as they would have been before your divorce.

*My private spaces blended with yours*
*We shared beds*
    *Tables*
      *Destinations*
*In one spirit, on one path*
*'Till words created distance*

*Now we walk on different paths*
*Yet we share the same legacy*
    *A child*
    *A life*
    *A soul*
    *A breath*
*Depending on our support*

*A life hoping for*
    *A family*
    *A father*
    *A mother*
    *Unlimited love*
    *Unlimited acceptance*

*A life that knows*
    *There are no sides*
    *And love is not finite*
    *And the world can be kind*

*How will we open our arms*
    *Our hearts*
    *Our spirits*
    *To our children?*

*We are the teachers...*
    *What will we teach?*

## Understanding Anger and Moving Beyond It

Most divorce lawyers will honestly tell you that they make the most money representing divorcing parties who harbor strong feelings of anger towards their ex-spouse. This anger is often what stimulates ongoing litigation. Frequently anger motivates not only the desire to get "a fair share" of property, but also to exact revenge and hurt the former partner. What purpose does this anger serve, and what causes it to linger in some people and not in others?

To answer these questions the origins of anger must be understood. Anger is a secondary emotion. There is always some underlying primary emotion—such as hurt, rejection, loss, a sense of injustice, or disappointment—that provokes the reactive emotion of anger. When a child darts in front of a car, fear for the child's safety drives a parent's angry scoldings. The jilted teenager's anger masks his jealousy. Perhaps the underlying feeling that is being masked is easier to define and express as anger. Reach below the feeling of anger and try to decide what is causing the anger. It may be rejection, fear, frustration, or a myriad of other emotions.

Whatever the original cause of the anger, the primary emotion is painful, and anger binds you to the pain. Divorce always involves pain, because everyone loses in a divorce. The loss may be your dream of the future swept out from underneath you. As one parent put it: "All my dreams were shattered. I felt I had to redefine everything that mattered to me." Or it might involve actual physical losses, such as leaving the family home, leaving the neighborhood and friends, or the reality of financial losses. These losses hurt.

No one goes into a marriage expecting to end up divorced. Otherwise they wouldn't marry in the first place. Most people marry with hopes, dreams, and idealistic beliefs about the shape their lives will take with the person they love. Entering into marriage automatically means that much of your individuality and identity is now going to be joined with another human being's identity. Marriage is a joining of two individuals to become a third identity, a couple, a partnership. This step requires a tremendous voluntary investment of the self, with the intent to love and give of yourself for a lifetime.

Giving yourself to another in a marriage involves devoting yourself to another person on physical, emotional, mental, and spiritual levels. Creating the intimate relationship of marriage involves the sharing of your most vulnerable and private self. You

> Dear mom and Dad, If Parents get divorced does that mean they will Stop fighting? PLEASE don't fight.
> Love your kid,

place an enormous amount of unspoken trust in your partner with the assumption that he/she will respect your vulnerability.

Unfortunately, when divorce is in its beginning stages, situations occur where each party hurts the other through not respecting the former trust which had once joined them. Any betrayal of trust wounds deeply, and a natural reaction to pain—physical or emotional—is to lash out at its source in an effort to stop the hurting. This is why many partners who once shared their most private selves will turn so completely against their marital partner. Sometimes the better the relationship has been in the past, the more disappointed and angry they feel. Their vengeance often matches their anguish. Many actually foster the mistaken belief that the only way to relieve the pain is to hurt the other person.

In this arena of pain and disappointment, couples who once shared their most private selves and joined together to create beautiful children wage bitter war against each other in messy courtroom dramas. We can choose healthier solutions.

Writing about your feelings may help you discover which feelings are fueling your anger so you can move beyond them. Any type of writing that helps you identify deeply felt emotions will also help you release the emotions and, in the process, aid your healing.

Once you determine that you want peace in your life and in your children's lives, it is a matter of committing yourself to this choice. The rest will follow in time.

There are other ways to sort through your emotions and motivations. Talk to a counselor. Find a friend who has also been through divorce and who has found a way to let go of anger. Whatever method suits you, take time to examine your motivations and explain your feelings to yourself. Act rather than react.

Don't be afraid to apologize when you've handled things badly. Apologizing doesn't mean caving in to abuse, conceding your point, or losing dignity. It means you are carving out space to be human and changeable. Being able to apologize when necessary will help you keep your emotional balance. Always being in the right is less important than healing. During a divorce everyone makes mistakes. Don't be too hard on yourself, or on others. I wrote the following lyric one day after I lost my temper. This apology helped build bridges for me, as well as being good therapy. It helped me let go. It helped me heal.

---

### Excuse Me

Something you never meant to do,
Made my jealous side burst through.
Angry words, sneering remarks,
A thought to hurt filled my heart.
It's hard to watch your dreams come true,
With someone else living them out for you.
A simple truth explains it all—
I built a home and watched it fall.

You've had somebody by your side;
I've been alone at night and cried.
Thinking of all the things I miss,
Needing a hug, a word, a kiss.
Sometimes I can't stop feeling sad,
Remembering so many things I had—
Even the love I want to show
No longer has a place to go.

I didn't prepare for things to end.
My path was straight without a bend.
I thought my future was all planned,
But now alone again I stand.
I never knew I'd have to start
A different dream inside my heart,
Or dam the feeling, deny I care,
And find another's love to share.

Excuse me if I cast you villain,
If I ladle out the blame.
Excuse me for expressing anger
As I pass around my pain.
It's still me, though I seem a stranger—
Another time I'll be myself again.

---

I later wrote a letter of invitation to my former husband and his girlfriend to have a "peace" dinner. I wanted to show my daughter that I could accept her father's new relationship and, by doing so, give her permission to do the same when she is ready.

*Dear Giff and Liz,*

*I would like to invite both of you to join Aimee and me for dinner on Monday night at Ferrantelli's. I hope that this can be a "peace" dinner so that we can all move forward in a healthy way.*

*As Giff has already noticed, Aimee seems to be showing some loyalty conflicts between the two of us. This is natural in a divorce situation, particularly when a third party is introduced. Most kids, including Aimee, want their family to remain as they knew it. It is common for them to feel angry about their family splitting up. They then look for someone to blame. I don't want her to blame anyone because it would hurt her relationship with one of her parents. Obviously we all agree that she needs the best possible relationship with each parent.*

*In my opinion, the best way to prevent her from feeling angry at either of us is to literally give her permission to show loyalty to both, regardless of the situation. If we can demonstrate this in a friendly way by all going out to dinner and sharing friendly conversation, she will observe that it is OK to accept the new scenario, because we are all doing so. I truly believe this will be in Aimee's best interest and I hope you agree.*

*I have been actively working at "letting go" of things the way I once knew them to be. Even though I slip at times, when it comes to Aimee I am clear about preserving the good feelings she has for both of her parents. If Aimee can see me accepting another woman in your life, Giff, then she will have an easier time doing so. At this point she is confused, and I think this dinner plan would help her along. I know it's hard for her and I want to help her with this, so please accept this invitation. If you have any better ideas let me know. I hope you agree that we should take action to help her make sense of the new situation.*

*You can be sure that I will not get angry because this is for Aimee and I can certainly control my feelings when it comes to her.*

*Also, I've been meditating on forgiveness for all of us, and moving out of my anger. It does no one any good, particularly me, to stay angry. For your information, I have noticed that my anger really rises when I feel that I have been lied to or treated disrespectfully. Although honesty might sting in the beginning, it helps to get through this in a more respectful and trustworthy manner. You have my permission to be honest. Please don't lie to protect my feelings any longer. Thank you both.*

*Thanks for considering this invitation. I'll check with you on this.*

> *Peace,*
> *Elizabeth*

## Victimized vs. Self-Reliant

How we perceive ourselves has a major influence on what we create and manifest in our lives. Therefore it is important to recognize a victim posture in divorce, as opposed to the empowering, self-reliant posture. What we believe to be true for us is what we ultimately draw into our lives and live out, over and over again. On the next page is a comparison of thoughts: one side is the victim position and the other is one of being empowered. It is your choice.

Parents are the only ones with the power to lessen the pain of divorce. If for no other reason than the child's sake, strive to communicate peaceably.

No matter how innocent the information may seem to you—it is uncomfortable for the child to be in the middle of your discussion.

| Victim Posture | Self-Reliant Posture |
| --- | --- |
| He/she did this to me. | This divorce is an event that happened to both of us. |
| The divorce is all his/her fault. | We both contributed to the divorce. |
| I'm the only one that knows this despair. | I am where I am because of my choices. |
| I'm alone in the universe. | If I look, I can find love and support from family, friends, and others. |
| Life is punishing me. | Life is a teacher. Each experience has a lesson. |
| My parents never prepared me for this. | My parents did the best they could; parents aren't perfect. |
| My dysfunction is a result of my childhood. | I can choose a path different from my dysfunctional childhood. |
| I'm not attractive enough. | I am enough, I am valuable, my personality radiates from within. |
| Who will want me at my age? | I can be forever young in my heart and soul. |
| I reached my physical peak ten years ago, and it's all downhill from here. | I can be attractive at any age, if I choose to be. |
| My dreams are shattered. I'll never trust again. | I can dream again. I can make new dreams. I can also learn to trust those who are trustworthy. |
| It's not fair. Why me? | I can choose my reactions to life's events. Some things I have no control over, but I can control my reactions. |

# Some Ground Rules for Communicating as Co-Parents

After a divorce most people experience difficulty setting up and sticking to new ground rules for communicating with their former spouse, who remains a parenting partner. Learning to communicate differently will feel awkward and unnatural at first. You may be repeatedly thrown off balance, but your skill at communicating peaceably will develop with time and practice.

The major task is to distance yourself from and unlearn the reaction patterns that developed during your marriage relationship. These are now so ingrained that they seem spontaneous. But your relationship as co-parents is very different. It has different rules, expectations, and boundaries.

The loving, intimate marital relationship you began with may have become untrusting, angry, and resentful. Habits of communicating may now need to evolve into a more formal and businesslike, less personal, relationship. To begin with, you may wish to agree to be as formal as possible.

- Conversation that before was intimate now should be courteous and businesslike.
- Where assumptions were once acceptable and commonplace, nothing can be assumed.
- What was unspoken and unwritten now must be explicitly agreed upon, often in written contracts.
- Where life was informal, now formal courtesies, structured interactions, meetings, specific agendas, and negotiations are the rule.
- Where once intense and erratic emotions prevailed, now even and balanced emotions must be the standard.
- Where once open disclosure was expected, now privacy is necessary.
- Where once there was open access, now there are time limitations and boundaries.

Your common concern—the basis for your new relationship—is your child's welfare. Divorce raises many new family problems to be dealt with. Some will be unpleasant and unsettling.

I recall one case from my years as a custody evaluator where the parents were making no effort to communicate. They were not on speaking terms, so the children had to serve as intermediaries, relaying "Mom says"—"Dad says" messages back and forth. Their adolescent daughter told her father that her mother simply couldn't afford school clothes for her, and so the father provided her with a clothing allowance. She told the same story of financial distress to her mother. It was not until the family met in mediation that either parent discovered how their hostility had doubled a daughter's wardrobe.

However, not all stories are as harmless. One fourteen-year-old told each parent she was spending the weekend with the other parent, knowing they never spoke to each other. She actually spent the weekend unsupervised at a friend's home. Communicating through the children is difficult at best and dangerous at worst.

For the sake of your children, you need to communicate regularly as co-parents. You can learn to communicate effectively and peaceably if you are determined to find a way.

## *Encourage Effective Communication by:*

- **Attentive Listening:** Acknowledge what the other person has to say. Don't interrupt. Hear each other out before responding.

- **Personal Statements:** Use "I" messages which reflect your feelings or attitudes. For instance: "I feel sad when the kids cry because they miss you. I would like to find ways for us to work together so we can address their feelings."

- **Restatements:** Validate the other person's statements by restating them in your own words. "It sounds as though you are sad about the children being upset and that you want the two of us to solve this problem together." Restating the message conveys your understanding, even if you do not necessarily agree.

- **Asking for Input:** Invite discussion of how to solve a problem. For instance: "Tom didn't make the football team, and he's really upset. Do you have any ideas how we can help him through this right now?"

- **Focusing on Your Child's Welfare:** Avoid discussing what is fair or convenient for *you*. Focus on the needs of the *child*. Let your conversation be prompted by the question, "What choice will serve the overall best interests of our child?"

## Parenting Meetings

I advocate a monthly meeting between parents to discuss pertinent issues that concern the child. If you can anticipate potential concerns, you will be more successful at shared parenting. Prepare the same way you would for a difficult business meeting. Focus on the child, not your emotions. Be courteous and businesslike.

### Guidelines for a Regularly Scheduled Parenting Meeting

1. Choose a time that is convenient for both of you. Be on time.

2. Meet in a public place, such as a restaurant or the library.

3. Limit the meeting to forty-five minutes at most. Emotions can flare if discussions become drawn out.

4. List what you plan to discuss. Bring all information related to the items on your list (child care schedules, school activities, performances, lessons, activities, copies of report cards, budgets, etc.).

5. Start with the topics you are most likely to agree on.

6. Stay on the topic at hand. Stick to business.

7. Write down dates and times and note any changes in normal procedure.

8. If it is necessary to consult the child for information before a decision, agree to continue discussing the topic at a later date.

9.   If you disagree, agree to drop the topic for several days. If you still can't agree, consult an unbiased third party.

10.   Listen attentively and consider the other person's viewpoint. You don't have to agree, but you should demonstrate respect.

11.   Bring up the past only if it relates to the child's present or future needs.

## Problem Solving

1.   Ground Rules:

  • Agree to find a win-win solution for the problem

  • No name-calling or insults

  • Speak one at a time; no interrupting

  • Listen to the other person

  • Tell the truth

  • Agree to mediation if necessary

2.   Apply formal problem-solving skills and procedures:

  • Each person presents his/her view on the topic.

  • Each listener indicates understanding by summarizing what the other person has said. (This summary does not mean you agree, but that you understand.)

  • Brainstorm solutions. Avoid "my solution vs. yours" power struggles by offering at least three solutions to every problem. (If possible, invite the child's input. Sometimes children generate great solutions.)

  • Choose solutions that best meet the needs of the child. Avoid purely personal objectives.

My good friend S. P. Romney often expresses his feelings through songs. His physical and spiritual artistry have contributed greatly to this book. The following lyrics, *Feeling is the Pathway to Healing*, are his.

### *Feeling is the Pathway to Healing*

*It takes both halves to make a whole.*
*They need not struggle for control.*
*Accept each equally and find,*
*Balance, strength and peace of mind.*

*When teardrops come, let them flow.*
*When laughter rises, let it grow.*

*Expressing anger helps you heal,*
*Accepting love can make it real.*
*Turning inward guides your learning.*
*Reaching out fulfills all yearning.*

*Allowing yourself to feel the pain*
*Opens you up to the joy again.*

*For every hurt feeling—there is healing.*
*S.P. Romney*

# 10
# *Difficult Divorces*

All divorces are difficult; some are more challenging than others. One purpose of this book is to argue for and support a child's continuing relationship with both parents regardless of the level of difficulty in the divorce. No matter how rocky the start you can still achieve the goal. I use the terms "co-parenting" and "shared parenting" because active parenting by both is the ideal situation for a child after divorce. However, I realize that shared parenting is rarely easy. Patience, courage, dedication, and persistent effort will be required. To make your plans work, you will also need to exercise empathy and understanding toward the other parent. As with any exercise, strength will build with regular effort.

What if you are doing your best to promote shared parenting, but the other parent is pointedly sabotaging your parent-child relationship? Do you sit back and allow the sabotage to continue? If you "fight back" is your partner likely to stop? Or will the fighting simply escalate with both of you feeling even more justified in being surly and uncooperative? Let me suggest some strategies for breaking out of the cycle of retribution.

1. Try communicating indirectly. If your ex-partner was unable to accept advice graciously from you during the marriage then she/he probably won't listen to you during or after a divorce. An alternative may be to enlist the support of someone your ex-partner respects. Perhaps a family member who has a

vested interest in the well-being of your child would be willing to "talk sense" to the obstructive parent.

The adversarial parent may be willing to hear from a friend or family member what she/he won't listen to from you. Your approach should be to describe the troublesome behavior of your ex-partner. But don't tattle-tale. Don't outline all the rotten things she/he does to hurt you or the child. Instead, provide objective, factual information to extended family about the needs of children whose parents divorce. Focusing on the needs of the child, not on either parent, will be more readily accepted. You might begin, "I've been reading that children do better after a divorce if they are kept out of their parents' conflicts and feel free to like and be with both parents."

The information from this book may help you convince those who are genuinely concerned for the child to think twice before condoning behavior aimed at alienating a child from one or the other parent.

2. Appraise the situation from the ex-spouse's perspective. Try to sense how they are feeling. If they are angry, they are likely to blame you. They may feel you have wronged them, and if they think you are completely happy, this causes more rage. The thinking may go something like, "You stole my hopes for the future, you disrupted my dreams for our children, and now you are walking away happy!"

3. Deal with negative feelings. Acknowledge that you are hurting and that you are feeling the pain of lost hopes and dreams. You both entered into your marriage with high hopes for happiness together and, although things have not worked out, admit that you never set out to cause the destruction of your mutual dreams. Admit that you are sorry that you are both hurting, and that you hope things will get easier for both of you.

4. Share information that is important to the child, regardless

My parents got divorced when I was 4, and it was really hard at first because when I was at home I'd miss my dad, and then when I went to his house, I'd miss my mom. It was very hard to get used to that.

—Annie, age 11

Acknowledge that this is a difficult time for everyone. Trying to get back at the person who hurt you only creates more pain for everyone.

Both parents should attend school plays and little league games. If you're the custodial parent, keep the other parent informed about your children's activities.

of the discord between the two of you. Show an attitude of trying to be more cooperative. When you take pictures, have two sets of prints made. Put together a photo album of the child for the other parent saying, "I thought you might enjoy having these photos in your home also." If applicable, order duplicates of school pictures for the other parent.

5. Inform the other parent of upcoming events that you think might be of interest. Give adequate notice so they can make the necessary arrangements to be there. The child should not suffer because of the parents' conflict. It is important to a child to see both parents sitting in the audience delighting in their accomplishments. However, if there is friction between the parents, prepare the child for the difficulties of deciding who they greet first after the performance. You might say, "After the performance, why don't you greet Dad first, and I'll find you when you're finished." This prevents  possible worry and concern.

6. Reevaluate your expectations. Visualize the quality of relationship you want in the long term with your children. Make each action and interaction lead in that direction, regardless of here and now or the other person's actions.

In time, a cooperative, non-manipulative attitude toward the other parent will be noticed. The other parent may not thank you, but your child will reap the benefits. As time goes by and the emotions decrease, the other parent may become more objective and appreciate your helpful approach. But the primary payoff in the long run will be the increased well-being of your child.

## Abandonment

In case the other parent abandons your child, your only recourse is to help your child cope with the immediate and long-term emotional repercussions. A therapist can help you understand the full

emotional implications of abandonment and help your child process feelings in a healthy way.

## Unvoiced Antagonism

Some parents find it difficult to be in the same room with each other. Parents who think that children do not feel that tension are fooling themselves. All children sense parental emotions, even if they can't verbalize what they are experiencing. Children who still need to be physically exchanged from parent to parent are particularly affected.

I remember one case where visitation with the mother was permitted only in my presence. During these "supervised visitation" sessions, the preschool child would spend half the session just getting used to being with her mother. Once the child felt comfortable, the mother would bring out a prepared activity—play dough, popsicle stick airplanes, or a coloring book and crayons for them to work on together. When I would return the child to the father, the child would show the father what he had made. Sensing her father's unvoiced disapproval, the child would take the project, tear, crumble, or break it, and scowling, jam it into the garbage can. She felt she needed to show her father that she wasn't pleased with her mother, either. Children learn to play roles that they think will please the parent they are with.

## Withholding Time from a Parent

Some custodial parents will interfere with the designated time-sharing schedule and actually withhold the child's time with the noncustodial parent. One frequently provided reason for this is "He didn't pay his child support! He doesn't deserve to see the children!"

One wrong action doesn't justify another, and this is typically

At first my dad couldn't come to see me because my mom would yell a lot about his not giving her enough money and stuff.
—Tiffany, age 9

"Children are part of the divorce process, but they are not divorced from their parents."

how the courts will view the matter. If there is a substantial, serious reason to stop a child's time with the other parent (i.e., you have knowledge that the parent takes the child to bars and has had three DUI convictions), inform your attorney and your local child protective services agency. Be prepared to back up your concerns with actual evidence. You will need to return to court to have the divorce decree modified.

## Reintroducing Time with the Other Parent

If a parent corrects the problems which prevented them from having free access to their child, there should be a gradual reintroduction of time-sharing.

In less extreme situations, where the parents' difficulties with each other caused the interference of time, it may be difficult for both parents to admit their error. Therefore, if you are the parent whose time with the child has been limited, acknowledging that you want to get things "back on track" for the child's sake can help.

For example, drop a note or leave a message that you noticed Johnny has developed a real interest in basketball lately, you were just given two tickets to a basketball game and would like to take him next Wednesday. Indicate that you'll have him home on time and that you'll make sure he gets his homework done before the game.

This approach clearly puts the interests of the child first. It is easier for a parent to agree to this type of an offer than to one that appears to benefit only the other parent.

In difficult divorces, the parties are clearly not interested in satisfying each other's desires. When there is disagreement and the court must resolve the case, try to reach a compromise. Even though the temporary arrangements you agree to may be far from perfect, at least you will know the children are not being sacrificed.

Children need parents who can find ways to communicate and create peace. Children feel the vibrations of tension and conflict.

## *Real Stories Reflecting Real Problems*

I have learned through hundreds of custody evaluations, there are always two sides, and both parties are right—according to them. While one side of a scenario can sound very convincing, it is better to continue listening and learning than to form immediate conclusions.

Growth through divorce occurs when both parties learn to listen, communicate, and look for solutions which validate everyone, but especially the children. When they make their judgments and form their perceptions, they must always remember their primary concern is the best interests of the child.

In the search for understanding, moving away from your own strong position long enough to consider things from the other person's perspective, is the first step to opening the door for compromise and settlement.

The following letters were written by parents with strong convictions who were expressing their feelings and positions in an attempt to settle their problems with their ex-partners. They have been included, with permission from the writers, to demonstrate the difficulty of parents' struggles. All the names have been changed to protect their current parenting relationships. Following each letter is a lesson that can be learned from the writer's experience. Learning from others who have gone before you may prevent unnecessary pain and heartache.

The first letter was written by a mother of four children to the father. She had consistently expressed a desire to communicate so that a "shared parenting" and a joint custody arrangement could be created. The father refused to participate in direct interaction, so communication broke down. This did not support the premise of "joint legal custody," which assumes the ability to communicate and make decisions on behalf of the children.

*Peter,*

*Having reflected extensively on the matters of our newly acquired lifestyle, I have come to the decision that joint custody is simply impossible. From the moment of separation, all the decisions concerning the divorce and the attorney's fees have been made by you, leaving me to pick up the pieces. At each step, I have expressed my preferred choices but your response has left me completely out of the decision-making process. In my attempts for a less lopsided process I have insisted on mediation as a resource; this you have dismissed too.*

*When I asked for help in scheduling vacations, you interpreted my requests, as you put it in your letter, as "a veiled power play on your part in our current attempt at direct negotiations . . ." You have accused me of using the children for my own gain and using guilt trips to take advantage of you. I simply shared information on the children's behavior and needs which I consider important for joint custody.*

*As to my requesting some modification to your vacation plans, and making yourself available when the kids are sick, I must assure you that the only reason I did it was because, at the time, I considered you the first resource to call upon when the children needed someone in addition to me. If this request seemed at all based on my needs it is because I have chosen to be there for the children through thick and thin. If I had been alone and considering only my needs, I can assure you that nothing would be expected of you as I am a self-sufficient and resourceful person.*

*Communication between us is less than effective. You assume underlying reasons for my reluctance to talk to you through your attorney, when I am only trying to build up our ability to communicate for future joint custody. Letter writing, messages through the phone, and direct dialogue have all failed.*

*I had great hopes that mediation could help us in building skills and creating at least a temporary bridge between us, but your response was always the same, "definitely not."*

*If I have to discuss all matters through your attorney as you said, how will we learn to communicate and be "co-parents?" Will we be calling our attorneys two years from now when we can't agree on new issues? I hope not! I think we need to put our feelings aside and work toward building a different relationship for the sake of our four children.*

*Unfortunately, this was emphasized in a more painful way last week with Sierra. When I took her to the doctor on Monday she was in excruciating pain with a serious bladder infection. I was not aware of the situation until late Friday when Sierra told me she took two bubble baths at your home to alleviate her previous discomfort, but had aggravated the condition. I immediately called you for more information and you told me that the discomfort had started on Wednesday! You were putting the responsibility of health issues onto a five-year-old child instead of telling me so that I could act.*

*I assume that none of this situation was intentional. It must be your unwillingness to improve our communication that is at the root of this unfortunate incident. The extent of your reluctance to communicate worries me.*

*It is for all these reasons that I see joint custody as a dream that cannot come true. Parenting together under a joint custody settlement requires a desire and an ability to work together. Since you left you have been playing a solitary game which is absolutely not appealing to me.*

*I hear your desire to co-parent and I willingly accept what I think is best for the children. I support your involvement and even your input in their lives. However, when it comes to making decisions together we are severely handicapped. Until now I have hoped and wished for joint parenting. Presently, I am resigned to and accept the responsibility of sole custody.*

*I regret that things have to be this way.*

> *Sincerely,*
> *Sara*

Let the power of forgiveness heal the pain of yesterday.

**Lesson To Be Learned: It is important to act in ways which are consistent with your desired outcome.**

The next letter was written by a father of two children who was seeking custody of his son and daughter. He had experienced numerous frustrations with visitation interference which involved false accusations against him. He spent over $40,000 defending himself and clearing himself. Eventually the children admitted that the incidents never happened, but that the stepsiblings had prompted the accusations because they didn't want the children to see their father. The children still loved their father and wanted a relationship with him, but they were torn between loyalties.

Children develop their self-esteem from their concept of both parents. When children are not permitted to feel good about both parents, their own self-esteem suffers.

*Dear Susan,*

*After a lot of thought about our children's best interests, I would like to make a settlement proposal to you. Throughout this entire process, all I wanted was to have a good relationship with Cassidy and John, Jr.—I love them with all my heart and I know that they love me. I want the chance to play an active role in their lives. I know in my heart that they will be happier growing up with the knowledge that they are loved by both their mother and their father.*

*In the past five years, I have had very limited contact with our children. This situation has hurt all of us. Each time I attempted to get time with them, there was some reason that visitation was denied, and I got very frustrated with being denied the opportunity to show love and interest to my children.*

*As I wandered through the legal system and learned about options for handling this, I was told that I should pursue custody. I felt that it was the only way to get the chance for a meaningful relationship with them.*

*Now that we are beginning a custody battle, I think about sweet little Cassidy and John and the tension and stress that they will both be exposed to from this. Fighting over custody will cause both of us to compete with each other. They are bound to feel the emotional strain from this. I don't want this for them. I want them to feel peace and love from both of us in their lives. I want them to know that they can love Mommy and Daddy. I want them to know that they don't have to choose between us.*

*Because of my concern for their emotional health, I am asking you to participate in settling this custody dilemma so that our children can be spared the pain. My sincere desire is that we can all go forward in a happy and productive manner. I know that this is possible. Please consider this, Susan. You are the mother of our precious children, and I want to make peace with you. I know it will be hard to put the past behind us, but we can do it if we choose to. And our children will be better off because of it.*

*With these things in mind, I am asking the following:*

*1. Put the custody evaluation on "hold" while we attempt to settle the visitation schedule and custody on our own.*

*2. Participate in mediation for the purpose of working out our time-sharing schedule for the children and other problems that we have concerning them.*

*3. Agree to have joint legal custody, with your home being the "primary residence," allowing you to still make all of the day-to-day decisions, but discussing the big things like school and serious medical problems with me. Joint custody would help me to feel I can have an active role in their lives as they grow up. I do not want to take them away from their other family either. I know the children love them and they love the children. I just want both of us to have the chance to be with them.*

*4. I would like to have at least the legal standard visitation schedule for standard visitation and I think that Cassidy, John, and I deserve at* least that. We could use this as a guideline when we go into mediation. Mediation would allow both of us to talk about the problems we have with custody and the schedule, and the mediator will help us to focus on the problem and reach some agreement instead of arguing about it through the court. I am willing to pay for a private mediator.

I think we owe it a shot to see if we can work these things out. I have the names of several expert mediators recommended by the courts. I have not spoken with any of them yet. I am just looking for the best qualified person who can assist us in reaching some agreement. Please consider it.

5. I would also ask that both of us say only positive things to the children about each other and that we don't put them in the position of feeling they have to choose between us. I know this stresses them out.

6. Also, I request that we follow up on the court recommended therapy so that we can resolve our emotional problems. I also ask that we include the other family members in therapy so that they know we are all honestly working to put the past behind us.

Feel free to call me or have your attorney call my attorney. I am anxious to hear from you.

I hope that you understand that I have asked all of these things with Cassidy's and John's best interests in mind. I love them as much as you do and I don't want to do anything to hurt them. I don't want to take the children away from you. I just want the chance to be a part of their world.

*John*

This was the father's final attempt to settle. It was not accepted. They have since gone through a child custody evaluation, including psychological evaluations of both parties. The children were still in the middle. The end result was very similar to what the father initially requested. Unfortunately, family members were forced to go through a very painful process, one which could have been avoided if both sides had compromised.

***Lesson to Be Learned:*** **Compromise is often necessary to safeguard the well-being of the children.**

The third letter of the group is by a father who is trying to discourage the brainwashing the other parent is inflicting on the children. He is also trying to implement the visitation order the court has provided and is returning to court to have the order enforced.

*Dear Cynthia,*

*The best thing that resulted from our marriage was five beautiful girls that belong to both of us. We did not love each other and, obviously, our marriage was not meant to be. You were just as unhappy with me as I was with you, and your parents were totally unhappy with our marriage from the start, but five years ago, you were able to go on and progress by remarrying.*

*It was difficult for me to accept the fact that my little girls would be raised with another man in the role of their father, in the house that I provided. But I allowed it because I wanted you to be happy and I wanted my girls to be comfortable in your happiness with Steven. I cared enough to allow you to go ahead and start a new life with Steven without any sort of bugging or harassment.*

*Well, three years ago, I was finally able to find someone to love and who loves me. Ever since I married Rebecca, you have not stopped harassing us by using my girls as playing pieces in what seems to be a "controlling" sort of game to you. You need to accept the fact that you and I were never happy and weren't meant to be together. I deserve the same courtesy I've given you.*

*The way I see it, the court has ordered me to pay child support, and has ordered you to allow me liberal visitation to coincide with my days off. I am completely current and timely in my child support of our five daughters and yet you don't allow me time with the children.*

*I love all five of them and want to see them as often as I can. I have done everything that the court has ordered of me and beyond. You have made a mockery of the court system by refusing to obey your part of the court orders. You have gone in contempt of court as you have not complied with any of the court orders legally, morally, or ethically.*

*I came up with the idea of visiting with Cami and Ann at their school during their lunch and recess time. I went there a few times, only staying for 15 or 20 minutes one day a week. Now, you have ripped that away too. I have asked for visitation many, many times and you have denied it. I've documented these incidents. I have witnesses that you have stated that the girls will never be allowed to come visit me ever again. I have tape recordings of phone conversations.*

*Why are you stopping the girls from seeing me? Why are you poisoning their hearts and minds against me? I am their Daddy! Why can't you leave your personal feelings out of it and allow me and my girls a normal relationship? What have you told them to have them turn and hate me as much as you do—and so abruptly? I deserve to at least know what you have told them. Is your hatred for me so great that it has blinded you from seeing that, by pulling the girls into it, you have caused damage to them emotionally? This is what causes people to have problems in their own family and have to have ongoing therapy when they are adults.*

*I don't understand your reasoning at all, but I am pleading with you to keep your personal feelings to yourself. As you are teaching our girls to be good and do the right things, please don't teach them to hate their own daddy!!!*

*If we can't see eye to eye, let's keep it between you and me. Let's not burden our kids with our problems. It's bad enough that they will have many obstacles to overcome in their lives. Let's not have them carry the weight of having to overcome ours, too.*

*I believe we need to come to some sort of reasonable agreement, because I can't just give up my girls. In my line of work [a police officer], I am here today and could be gone tomorrow. I don't think I'm asking too much from you. Please allow my girls to feel free and at ease to associate with me.*

*I have faith in the court and the justice system and the new laws that have just been passed and I feel it is time that we go before the judge. I am coming to the court with my hands clean, having complied with all that the court ordered. I am prepared to point out your noncompliance of court orders. I am also prepared to point out your obligation as a mother. You have deprived my mother of knowing her five granddaughters. My mother has never received even any pictures of my girls since we've been divorced. You have deprived my girls of knowing the most wonderful woman in this world.*

*Cynthia, if your intent in all of these actions has been to hurt me, you have succeeded many times over!! But, you see, there are no winners in these situations—only losers. The children lose the very most. So, please stop! Stop hurting me. Stop hurting you. But, most important of all, please stop hurting our five beautiful girls.*

> *Sincerely,*
> *Roger*

***Lesson to Be Learned:* When one side has to be the "winner" the battle never ends.**

This last letter was written by a parent, resigned to divorce who had reached a healthy point in her healing. She had realized that striking out at her former partner created more problems and had identified that her anger was related to rejection.

*Tom,*

*Most of all, what I would like is a peaceful parting. Obviously, you have made it clear that our marriage is over. I will no longer fight this.*

*I ask that you respect me and tell me the truth as we go our separate ways. I won't be asking about Sherri because I can no longer allow myself to care. It's a waste of my energy and time. I need to move on.*

*I also request that you do not give me mixed messages about your intentions. This only confuses me and causes me to delay in the moving on process. Simply put, no more sex.*

*I am going to start dating again very soon just for the purpose of getting distracted and having some fun. The last few months have been a burden on me. I need to rejoin the living.*

*We need to share in more of the responsibilities for Brittney and Ryan. I*

> The bottom line is you might get divorced, but don't divorce your kids.
> —Kristy, age 13

*will let you come into the home every other weekend for your time with them and I will go elsewhere. At least on a temporary basis, this would be the least disruptive thing for them. I would hope that you could start this weekend, if not, the weekend we get back.*

*We will be in New York for six days. It is my hope that you will be mainly responsible for them during the evenings prior to our departure. I have many things to get ready for a meeting back there and will need the time to prepare for this.*

*I am making a sincere effort at being courteous and gracious about the separation and I will do my best to consider your feelings. I ask for the same level of concern. We have fought enough and it is now time to move forward in a cooperative attitude.*

*I apologize for the rude remarks made in reference to you and Sherri. I felt extremely hurt and rejected and acted out of my pain. I don't anticipate doing this anymore. I was still in disbelief that you were in love with another woman. I have finally accepted that it's over between us.*

*There must be better experiences waiting for me if I only give time a chance, which I'm now willing to do.*

*Peace,*
*Denise*

**Lesson to Be Learned: An apology clears the pathway to begin again.**

Below is a statement from a mother who allowed her children to live with the father, although she maintained legal custody.

*Following my divorce in 1982, for many reasons my four sons lived with my ex-husband, David and his second wife, Kathy, for what was supposed to be a few short months. Months turned into years. Even though we lived in different states I saw my sons often. Although I retained full custody, I gave financial help, food, and clothing to help out whenever I could. Kathy was tentative towards me at first, but as she came to see that my interest lay solely with the welfare of the boys, our relationship blossomed into full friendship. Sometimes I'd visit, and she and I would even go out to eat where we often discussed how to mutually raise the children. At one point Kathy said, "Isn't this strange? I've really tried to dislike you because you're the ex-wife and that's what society says. But instead I guess we've made our own rules and its wonderful to have an ally!" I loved Kathy for trying to be good to my sons, knowing she also had children to take care of from her first marriage; it was truly a blended family. We had an unspoken rule not to discuss Kathy's husband (my ex-husband) and he in turn granted a grudging respect for our dual mothering.*

*Eventually, however, the question of custody came up. It didn't take long for it to become a heated debate between David and me. Fortunately, Kathy stayed out of it. But the end result was to see a mediator.*

*The three of us sat in uncomfortable silence in the mediator's waiting room. Kathy and I couldn't look at each other. It was as if the last couple of years hadn't happened. The mediator took David in alone to interview while Kathy and I exchanged awkward glances. Finally, Kathy said, "I feel like a glorified babysitter. I feel like all this time you've just been using me so you could go off and lead a single life." I was so stunned I couldn't speak. What had happened to all those times discussing school work, discipline, and mutual child raising? I replied, "Kathy, you know that isn't true. I know you know I love the boys as much as you do. Weren't we helping each other?" She didn't answer. "And Kathy, didn't you say you loved me?" As she looked up with tears in her eyes, I felt my own eyes well up. With tears running down our cheeks, we hugged and laughed and the love between us immediately mended the rift. David eventually admitted in mediation that one of the members of his family had made him fear I would take the boys away without warning, out of revenge. Knowing this, I easily signed an agreement stating my willingness to allow my boys to stay with their "new" family unless all agreed it was best to change the arrangement at some future time. Kathy and I went back to mutually raising human beings, but with one significant difference—a deep-felt love that has grown in spite of obstacles.*

**Lesson to Be Learned:** **Love can be stronger than society's labels.**

As hopeful as I am when I start the mediation of a divorce case, there are extreme situations where divorcing parties simply cannot reach resolution.

In one case, the judge had ordered the parents to come to me to settle their visitation disputes. They had been to nine therapists in the community during the past three years. They claimed they were further away from a solution than ever. After two mediation sessions it became clear that the reason they were so far away from resolving their difficulties was that they were both so extremely invested in maintaining their dispute with each other. Each party was so convinced he or she was right, that neither would give an inch. They stated it was the "principle" of the matter that was so important, regardless of the need to resolve the issues at hand.

Although I pointed out to this couple that their disputes were harming the children, their investment in winning was so strong that they continued to minimize and rationalize that it wasn't *that* bad for their children. They actually convinced themselves that their children were coping fine. In reality, what the children were doing was simply "checking out." They could not deal with the trauma of their parents' feuds (which involved police intervention at one point). They simply withdrew. The price of this withdrawal created greater emotional distance between the children and their parents.

When the parents finished their court-ordered sessions of mediation, they went back to court to keep fighting. The last I heard, nothing had changed. This was an extreme situation but one that carries a clear message.

*Lesson to Be Learned:* **Sometimes it is more important to stop fighting than to be "right."**

> Even if my parents are divorced, I still need a Mom and a Dad.
> —Jared, age 12

## One Last Word about Difficult Divorces

### Abuse

I have dealt with many dysfunctional families where spousal/child abuse was present. In some of these situations the divorce was a relief for both the parent and the child. If this is the case for you, it is advisable to seek counseling for yourself and the child. It is important to deal with the pain so the abuse is not carried forward into your new lives. Not dealing with pain gives it power to direct other decisions that you make. The trauma of physical and emotional abuse needs to be dealt with, or it tends to become buried deep inside. The anger and pain does not go away until it gets attention.

There are types of abuse situations where it may be necessary to cautiously limit the contact between children and the other parent. The guiding principles in these cases is to consider the best interests of the child and to get professional, therapeutic support.

Children need both parents, yet they also need to be protected. It is sometimes difficult for a parent who is close to the situation to assess what might be appropriate for a child.

If you have an abusive situation, contact a therapist who specializes in issues of children and divorce visitation. Also, alert your attorney about your concerns and be prepared to give evidence supporting your suspicions.

# *11*
## *Redefining the Family*

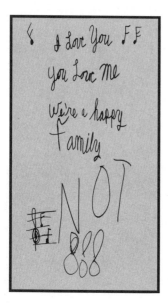

Even in cases of divorce or separation, a child can have a meaningful relationship with each parent and extended family members if given the opportunity. Sometimes anger motivates parents, and even extended family members to erect walls that deprive a child of the chance to further these relationships. At times this is done in the child's best interest (abuse, etc.) but at other times such action is motivated by hurt and anger. Many divisive deeds are done in the name of love and then reconsidered and regretted once the wounds have healed.

A child is born with two parents, four grandparents, aunts, uncles, and cousins. A divorce proceeding simply ends a marital relationship; it does not end a child's parental or extended family relationships.

A child does not come from a "broken home." Following a divorce, he has a restructured family. As parents, you have the opportunity to redefine your family for your child. Extended family relationships should be maintained and encouraged. Beyond that, new relationships with stepparents and extended stepfamilies can multiply the opportunities for love in your child's life. Love is not a finite substance; children of divorce can and will experience love from many significant adults in their world when they are given the encouragement and emotional permission to do so.

Children will wonder about their extended family if they're

not given the chance to know them. In certain cases, a child may need to have supervised time with adults who have problems. However, in many divorce situations one parent may grudgingly withhold access to the other parent's extended family simply because they view the family unit as an extension of their ex-spouse.

This type of behavior usually backfires on the custodial parent in later years. When a child grows old enough to understand that they have not been permitted to know the other half of themselves, they often get angry at the parent who interfered with this opportunity.

Remember the good times and talk about them with your children.

Consider your own childhood. Did you wonder what made your grandparents do the things they did? Did you assume certain things about them based on the perception you had of them during your formative years? Did this perception change as you grew old enough to recognize them for who they really were?

As people age, they have a tendency to grow on you. Their special and unique traits are a part of their history. These are the very things that go into a child's memory bank of "fond experiential memories" treasured forever. My own memories include: the old pine rocking chair Granny rocked me to sleep in, the recognizable smell of Grandpa when he was taking me on a fishing trip, smelling chocolate chip cookies in the oven when I walked into Aunt Mary's house, the tears of Aunt Kathleen when she suffered another broken heart, and the united grief when my mother died. For better or worse, these memories were stored and banked. They are a part of my history.

They are fond memories in spite of the sadness they may bring. They are memories of connecting with other members of my family, and they cause an emotion like no other emotion. The blood that binds family members together is thick and it's difficult to dilute. We need to respect that fact in making decisions about children in a divorce. Have a good explanation for the choices you make concerning your child's extended family. Be honest with yourself and others, because the truth always surfaces.

My daughter wonders about certain members of her extended family. I tried to protect her from relatives involved in situations that were too difficult to explain or understand. Some of these people have since passed on, and she asks me, "Why didn't you let me meet them?" She only heard stories and she wishes she could have at least seen for herself. As a parent, I recognize that she wouldn't have seen the same things that I saw, because her experience would have been completely different. I often ask myself the question, "What did she gain from my interference?"

Balancing caution with genuine concern is a delicate task, especially challenging in the throes of divorce. In the midst of broken hearts and shattered dreams, it's easy to throw many potential memories away. After all, you certainly don't want your child to suffer in the same way you suffered.

Recognizing the different variations of suffering is important. In a divorce, there are potentially four grandparents who also suffer wounds of shattered dreams. Their heartache also needs to be acknowledged and resolved. Although many states have laws outlining legal rights of a grandparent in a divorce, there are still many other states that refuse to acknowledge that grandparents have any right to be with their grandchildren after the parents divorce. Therefore new laws need to be considered to keep up with the consequences and reality of divorce in this country.

## Reaching out to Your In-laws and Other Extended Family

In the beginning of many divorces there are high emotions. This pain is often shared with family, friends, and basically anyone

The best way to suppose what may come is to remember what is past.
—George Seville

My child has a legacy. She has a family tree.
For her to know this, it's up to me.

who will listen. Things are said about how "she/he did this to me." Often when you're dumping your emotional garbage you release some of the pain and feel better. But you may not consider how this information will affect the person you're telling. As they listen, they may be thinking, "I can't believe he did that! How could a person be so insensitive and ruthless to his wife and children?" Impressions are formed and assumptions are made. Sometimes they are based on fact, but more often than not the impressions are made based on one person's emotional experience, which is not an objective evaluation.

It is to be expected that you will share some information about your former spouse in the heat of anger or from the despair of a broken heart. It is important to remember the people you vented to so that you can straighten things out once your emotions subside and you choose the best possible course for you and your children. If there are people holding a misperception of your former spouse based on something you said, then it becomes your responsibility to correct that.

This is especially important when these people are extended family members who interact with your children. If they believe that you were wronged by your former spouse, they will have a difficult time remaining neutral and supportive of the children's relationship with that other parent. Children often hear negative comments about their parents in those circumstances.

Well-intentioned adults don't understand how it hurts children to hear, "Your dad's a loser. Your mom is better off without him. He never did anything for your family except create problems." Even if children agreed with these statements in their own minds, it still hurts to hear other people talk that way about a parent, of whom they are an extension.

One teenager I worked with said: "My mom is irresponsible, she's always late; sometimes she doesn't even show up and it

Keep your criticisms and anger toward the other parent away from the children. Ask your extended family and friends to do the same. Tell them it's a necessary respect that your children deserve.

makes me mad and I say things about her, but I won't let anyone else talk bad about her. I can say those things because she's my mom, but other people can't say them because they have no right. If someone else says something bad about her, I defend her."

This type of loyalty is common with children and teenagers. It is unspoken that within a family everyone is somehow connected and they can talk about how someone affected them, but outsiders don't have that same right.

Considering these facts, it is important to make your intentions clear to anyone who interacts with your children who may have been "coaxed to your side" during the divorce. You need to let them know that your children deserve to have the best possible relationship with each of their parents with the least amount of interference from others. Request that these other adults join you in this commitment by not bad-mouthing either of you and allowing the children to speak openly about both parents when they want to.

Too many children of divorce are exposed to negative comments about a part of themselves (their mother or their father), and they quietly carry this hurt in their hearts. We can help their hurts heal by acknowledging and correcting our errors of judgment. Apologies clear the path for peace and for trust.

This is a letter I wrote to my husband's parents following our divorce. They had always been loving and kind to me, and I wanted to show respect for that by sharing my thoughts and feelings. It also proved to be a necessary part of my healing process. Depending on the situation, some form of a letter of explanation to your former in-laws might be worth considering.

> *Dear Mom and Dad,*
>
> *Today it's Giff's birthday and another moment to reflect on him and his spirit. It's been a tough ten years but tough times bring tremendous opportunities for growth. The best growth comes when we face circumstances that force us to look at ourselves and affirm who we are. I have*

*Teens often feel a black and white sense of right and wrong and may attempt to place all the blame for the divorce on one parent.*

*much to be grateful for in this way. And I believe that I offered Giff enough confrontation to look at himself and deal with his frustrations. I needed Giff to have some breakthroughs and he needed me to have the same type of breakthroughs.*

*Thank you for hanging in there through the years and listening to us as we struggled through our relationship and challenges. I don't think I could have designed a more supportive type of family. I believe that on a spiritual level Giff and I needed the lessons our relationship would teach us. Now it is time to step back from the front line and absorb the lessons and incorporate them into living.*

It's possible to shift a romantic love for a former partner to a love of respect and appreciation.

*In the process, I gained a bonus I never expected or thought possible. Another family—one that stands behind each other through thick and thin, and knows the meaning of unconditional love. Your family lives it, day to day. The jokes and fun abound, but underneath all of that, there is true commitment for each and every person. It is just understood. What better gift could a family, or parents, provide? What comfort it brings. I believe in faith and the goodness of the human spirit. It thrives in your family.*

*Thanks for including me in your precious circle of loved ones. What a nest to belong to! Each and every person in the family has a unique gift to offer and it is a rare privilege to know them for who they are. I honor this.*

*I love you both and thank you again. I will always love Giff; he has become a part of me, and I a part of him. We have completed the intense part of our work together, although we still have some lessons waiting in the wings. Somehow, I think the waters will not be as turbulent from here on.*

*His next life experience will include his new girlfriend, Liz, I'm sure. Because she has been good for Giff and helped him in ways that I never could, I know that your hearts will open to her as well. She loves the good in him, and helps him to achieve a calm and peace that was always lacking with him and me. Little do you see what he puts out to the world without recognition. Life has a way of balancing itself. He still comes to the rescue of those who suffer today; his work crew is made up of Native Americans, Hispanics, and others who are trying to make an honest living. He gives them the chance to feel good about themselves, and this is even more important than the money. It goes a long way in helping them feel successful. He befriends those who struggle and that is where the true spirit of living is experienced, the joy of giving and receiving.*

*You gave birth to Giff thirty-seven years ago today; you know him. He has a very good heart struggling to find a way to fit into this complicated world. Sometimes I think he sees too clearly what is, and this causes him to be a cynic. I think time will level this out. I often feel that his Grandma Fran is with him, and so does he. That type of presence can be a powerful influence. His heart is being softened in the process so that he can see the big picture. Grandma Fran is there, and so is his girlfriend. Because we all love Giff, we welcome what it will take to bring him peace and happiness.*

*The true love of Giff's life is Aimee and I get tears thinking about their bond. It will always have the opportunity to thrive and you can know that I will never interfere with that. On the contrary, I will do whatever I can to promote it.*

*Times are challenging for her now. It is hard to see your family split apart. Our love and commitment will see her through it. The support of her extended family has been felt many times over. Thank you. I know that even when she doesn't seem to be receptive, it is going into the experiential memory bank. This type of memory never goes away.*

*I love you both and can't begin to thank you for the love you send my way. I feel it and it makes me cry. Even now, the tears are flowing. But tears can be the expression of a fountain overflowing, and my internal fountain is pouring over with warmth and gratitude.*

*Love and Peace,*
*Elizabeth*

## The Caretaker Role

In 1993, I attended a national conference titled "Assuring A Child's Right to Two Parents." This topic drew a strong contingent of "fathers' rights" advocates. In fact, about seventy-five percent of those attending were male, an unusually high percentage.

For me, the nationally acclaimed speakers, innovative workshops, and stimulating discussions were all helpful, but I was moved by the intensity of the emotions of fathers, most of whom had come because they wanted the right to be involved in the lives of their children. Throughout the conference, I heard story after story from fathers who were unfairly denied access to their children—everything from fabricated sexual abuse allegations to bad faith relocation (a mother moving from state to state to keep a father from easy or regular contact with his child).

These memories jostle in my mind with other conferences where single mothers have described struggles to make ends meet without essential financial support from a spouse. In my practice

I have also listened to mothers describe their children's disappointment when a father shrugs out of promised time with them.

After divorce both men and women run into roadblocks of many kinds, which frustrate their intentions to be good parents. This chapter maps some new routes around the obstacles that stand in the way of redefining family life to match both the *hard reality* of our situations and our *best hopes* for our child's welfare.

## Beyond Gender Bias

Is there a gender bias in either custody or support decisions? Current statistics on outcomes for custody decisions clearly show that the courts still assign mothers custody in the large majority of cases.

How does the court go about making these decisions? A major factor in custody decisions is determining which parent was the "primary caretaker." The primary caretaker is assumed to have both more competence and a closer bond with the child because of their daily care. Primary care responsibilities include feeding, diapering, getting up at night with them, getting them ready for school, helping with homework, taking them to the doctor, arranging for babysitters and transportation, getting them to bed, arranging birthday parties, and so on.

Even when both parents are employed full-time outside the home, it is unusual to find two parents who actually share these primary care responsibilities on an equal basis. In most cases the mother assumes the primary caregiver role.

Attorneys frequently tell fathers who desire custody that they need to prove the mother "unfit" in order to win custody. I sincerely hope that this legal attitude is changing. However, the standard legal approach to winning custody for a father has not been to prove his competence as a custodial parent, but to list reasons why the mother is unfit for her natural role.

There are, in fact, support groups for mothers who have lost or given up custody because of the attitude that no "normal" mother could "give up" her children. In contrast, no one questions a father after a divorce as to why he "gave up" his children. Finances and strong traditional, societal expectations explain why fathers are not seen in the primary caregiver role as often as mothers.

For a number of years, a Utah statute referred to as the "Tender Years Law" mandated that mothers were automatically awarded custody of children if they were under the "tender years" of age five. It was assumed that maternal care was naturally better than paternal care during these young years. This law has since been challenged and overturned. Most states now have laws requiring that there be no gender preference in custody decisions.

However, even though the legal system has nominally changed the laws to exclude gender bias, mind-sets and attitudes have not changed concurrently. Judges are people. Most of them were raised in traditional family settings that influence their thinking about which gender should be the custodial parent, especially when both parents are competent and all other factors seem equal.

The process of nurturing life is the most profoundly transforming experience in the range of human possibilities.
—Dorothy Dinnerstein

One refreshing change emerging in some court jurisdictions is determining the "best interests of the child" on the basis of which parent will be most likely to encourage the child's relationship with the other parent. After years of research and ongoing time-sharing problems, it has become widely accepted as critically important that the custodial parent not only *facilitates* the other parent's relationship with the children, but actually *encourages* the relationship. After all, being a caretaker includes caring for the relationship the child has with their other parent. If this responsibility becomes expected of parents by the courts, and parents are held accountable to it, then theoretically the number of custody and time-sharing disputes should decrease, and everyone will benefit. Many of these problem cases return to the court out of sheer frustration at not being allowed, or encouraged to participate in a child's life—simply because the adults were no longer married.

> It is crucial to children that both parents play a significant, healthy role in their lives.

Society in general is recognizing the importance of the father role to children. Children who grew up without their fathers are vastly over-represented in juvenile detention centers, state prisons, and inpatient psychiatric hospitals, and are generally at higher risk for poor overall adjustment.

My personal and professional perception is that there is a resurgence of desire and interest on the part of fathers across the country to be more than providers. Most fathers want to be a significant part of their children's lives, whether in a home where the parents are married or in a divorced situation. The popularity of the movie *Mrs. Doubtfire* is undoubtedly due to the chord it struck for many who are concerned for the involvement of fathers in the lives of their children. The story clearly shows how the children needed their father, and how he needed his children. In the father's words, "I'm addicted to my children."

What makes a happy marriage? It is a question which all men and women ask one another. The answer is to be found, I think, in the mutual discovery, by two who marry, of the deepest need of the other's personality, and the satisfaction of that need.
—Pearl S. Buck

## Could Some Divorces Be Prevented?

Even after my own divorce, my opinion on this matter is that if more couples practiced "shared parenting" during marriage, the divorce rate would decline. Partners would appreciate more fully each other's contribution to the relationship and to the children, and feel less resentful about one partner doing a disproportionate amount of the parenting and household duties. Consequently, one partner would not feel as fatigued and there would be more energy for shared extracurricular activities, which could increase the couple's intimacy.

The practice of shared parenting during the marriage would strengthen the family bonds between the child and both parents. Strengthening the bonds between parents could make divorce less likely. Within a strong family unit, it is less likely that a partner will feel the need to see if the grass really is greener on the other side of the marital fence.

I have often said that if more couples understood the problems they must deal with due to their divorce, they would probably work harder on solving their marital problems. Many parents have actually expressed this when the reality of divorce sets in. The financial and logistical problems of setting up two households, dealing with parental boyfriends and girlfriends and consequent remarriage, juggling each parent's time-sharing schedule with their children, blending the children into a new family, facing possible court problems involving child support and time-sharing matters, and so on, are mind-boggling. The sheer complexity of the problems inherent in divorce make many marital problems seem manageable in comparison.

If divorced couples were honest about it, I think many would report that the grass isn't always as green as they expected it to be on the other side. Divorcing couples spend a vast amount of mental, physical, emotional, financial, and spiritual energy just to get through their divorce and cope with necessary changes. If this same amount of energy were applied to dealing with relationship issues within the marriage, there would possibly be a great improvement in the relationship, and less need for divorce.

This hypothesis is not based on any scientific data, it is merely a working premise to be more fully explored later. The intent of this book is to help parents feel empowered to help themselves and their children get through divorce in a healthy way, once the decision to divorce has been made.

This section was not written to cause any person feelings of guilt for choosing to divorce, but for two other reasons:

First, there are a certain percentage of individuals who are undecided about whether they should divorce, and they are studying the subject to help them decide. Possibly this section could serve as a motivator to do some relationship repair work and prevent a divorce.

Secondly, society must decide whether the reality and the consequences of a 50 percent divorce rate which has been flourishing in our country for the past decade, are acceptable. There are many implications of what has been coined as the "breakdown of the family." I believe we can create programs and attitudes that strengthen family relationships but only after looking at all sides of the situation. As one divorcing parent put it: "Divorce is a bad situation. It's not something you wish on yourself or your children. Once you're in the midst of it, emotions seem to take on a life of their own and it's up to us as parents to manage our emotions as best we can so that our children are not subjected to further trauma."

In fairness, there are many marriages that end after careful consideration by both parties. Indeed, the decision to divorce in

Children need to feel emotionally connected to both of their parents.

Biologically, men become fathers and women become mothers at the moment of their first child's birth. But only through daily care, and in sustained emotional engagement in their children's lives, do fathers and mothers become parents in the generative sense.

—Daniels and Weingarter, *Sooner or Later: The Timing of Parenthood in Adult Lives* (1982)

those cases is one that will move both parties in a more positive direction. A decision to divorce makes sense when it increases the personal contentment of both parties, which in turn provides children with happier and more emotionally available parents.

Society must create and implement policies that promote and encourage the involvement of two parents, regardless of family structure. The benefits for society will be felt in many ways, such as saving millions of dollars now spent collecting delinquent child support. Research clearly shows that the frequency of child support payments is directly linked to the level of involvement and influence a parent has in his or her child's life (Braver, 1993 and U.S. Census Bureau data). Simply put, maintaining the involvement of the noncustodial parent will automatically increase the child support payment frequency. When this happens, the child benefits, the parents benefit, and society benefits.

Growth is often accompanied with the sadness of letting go.

# Part II

by Elizabeth Dalton, J.D.

*12*

# *The Legal System*

Resolving divorce issues through the legal system can be a challenging process. Divorces are treated as civil lawsuits in most states, and are therefore adversarial. The adversarial process works in many areas of the law, but it simply was not designed with the best interests of families and children in mind. Often the legal process itself causes conflicts before, during, and after a divorce.

Fortunately, many legislators and judges today are working to reform the family law system in our country and make it more "family friendly." The introduction of divorce education and mandatory mediation programs has helped families learn how to minimize conflict during the divorce process. When conflict is minimized or avoided, children have a better chance of making a healthy adjustment to their parents' divorce.

Your court may use the word "visitation" to describe your time-sharing arrangements with your children, but I have deliberately chosen not to use the term "visitation" in this book. I believe that time with your child is much more than a visit and that parenting takes place by spending time with a child. I have seen the confusion on a child's face when they are told that they are going to visit a parent, but all they have ever experienced is living with that parent. In the instant that a child is told they are going to visit a parent, they begin to buy into the mistaken belief that the divorce has created a situation where they live with one parent and visit the other. This is an extreme disadvantage for the child

Minimizing the battle helps the child win, which means everyone wins.

and the visiting parent to overcome. Divorce is difficult enough without imposing negative terms on the new structure of the family.

Some judges across the country now refer to visitation as time-sharing in their courts. Hopefully every court will eventually establish "family-friendly terms" when speaking about divorce. This change alone will certainly decrease the perceived hostility that many noncustodial parents feel when they go before the court. But most importantly, children will still have the opportunity to believe that they truly have two parents.

During a divorce proceeding, several legal issues regarding parenting and finances must be resolved. During a time of crisis in their lives, parents are required to make critical decisions with long-term consequences. It is all too easy to make impulsive and hasty decisions that are motivated by guilt, anger, vengeance, or a desire to end the divorce quickly. Try to remember that people make their best decisions when they can put their emotions aside, become informed about the issues, focus on objective criteria, and consider all possible solutions.

> If you have never been involved in the legal system before, the experience may leave you bewildered, confused, and frustrated.

You may be tempted to ask attorneys, counselors, friends, or family members to simply "tell you what to do." Resist the temptation. When you allow someone else to make parenting and financial decisions for you, you give up control of your future to someone who is less knowledgeable and less concerned about both your needs and your family's. The best resolution of your parenting and financial issues is your own.

You need to maintain the role of decision maker in your divorce. Your attorney is your adviser, helping you understand legal principles and recommending strategies for conflict resolution. It is *your* job to make the decisions.

If you have never been involved in the legal system before, the experience may leave you bewildered, confused, and frustrated. The purpose of this section is to prepare you for making those decisions by informing you about the parenting and financial issues you might face and helping you understand your options.

*If there are contested issues, animosity, and mistrust in your divorce, the financial cost can be significant.*

## Common Legal Questions about Divorce

### How Much Does It Cost?

The financial cost of divorce depends on several factors. If there are contested issues, animosity, and mistrust, the financial cost can be significant. If you and your spouse can work cooperatively to resolve issues outside of court, the cost is manageable.

Court appearances, and preparation for those appearances in legal pleadings and briefs, cost money. Generally, the attorney's fees associated with negotiating a settlement will be less than the fees associated with appearing in court to present an argument.

Don't ignore the emotional costs. A divorce is one of life's most stressful and painful experiences. Extended legal battles only intensify conflict, and conflict increases the emotional harm to children.

## *Should I Seek Counseling?*

There are many painful, emotional issues that result from marital disharmony, separation, and divorce. Counseling can help you understand the issues and point the way towards healing. Often counselors can refer you to support groups, books, and other resources that further promote the healing process.

Be selective when choosing a counselor. There are many different styles and approaches to therapy. Ask your attorney, your friends, your church leader, or your family for references. Often health insurance will cover all or part of the cost.

## *How Do We Resolve Our Divorce Issues Legally?*

In either a contested or uncontested divorce, mediation is worth considering.

Generally, there are two ways to obtain a divorce through the legal system: by entering either an uncontested or a contested proceeding.

An uncontested divorce proceeding is also known as a "default divorce," which means that both parties have reached an agreement on all issues. The judge will sign a decree of divorce based on either a complaint or petition or a settlement agreement.

Settlements are typically negotiated outside of court, either before or after the complaint is filed. Parties can reach settlement agreements either on their own, with attorneys, or with the assistance of a mediator.

A mediator is an impartial facilitator who helps divorcing parties to resolve their parenting and financial conflicts. Mediated resolutions are often more sensitive to the specific needs of the family than are court-imposed resolutions. Therefore, in either a contested or uncontested divorce action, mediation is worth considering.

In an uncontested divorce, when a court appearance is required, only one party typically attends. Usually the time spent in court is short, and it involves giving testimony to establish the jurisdiction and grounds for the divorce. The court then enters a decree of divorce or a judgment dissolving the marriage.

In a contested divorce proceeding, one or more issues of the divorce are in dispute. Both parties are required to file pleadings that present their points of view. Attorneys may negotiate settlements or argue each party's position to the court. Attorneys will also conduct a discovery process to gather documents and other evidence relevant to resolving the disputed issues. The court will make rulings resolving all issues that are not settled at court hearings or at a trial.

## Can the Court Enter Temporary Orders before the Decree of Divorce Is Entered?

Often one party will seek immediate relief in the form of a temporary order after the divorce complaint or petition is filed. A temporary order from the court may be obtained to seek a restraining order, temporary custody, interim time-sharing, temporary spousal or child support, payment of attorney fees, or possession of a home.

It is important to be truthful and to give full disclosure of all information that may be relevant to your divorce proceeding.

## What Happens during the Discovery Phase of Divorce Litigation?

After a complaint or petition is filed in a contested proceeding, the attorneys begin a phase called discovery. In this phase, attorneys use a variety of methods to gather information that will help to resolve the financial and parenting issues. Discovery procedures include requests for documents, requests for admissions, interrogatories, and depositions.

Discovery may be informal or formal. Cost-conscious attorneys will try to gather informally as much information as possible. During informal discovery, an attorney may ask for information by telephoning the opposing counsel or asking you to gather documents and other information. In formal discovery, pleadings must be served on the opposing party.

Both sides will have access to all relevant information in order to prepare for trial and negotiate settlements. It is important to be truthful and to give full disclosure of all information that may be relevant to your divorce proceeding.

*Divorce decrees bind both parties to certain obligations and are enforceable by the court.*

## What Does It Mean to Have a Bifurcated Divorce Proceeding?

In some states, it is possible to separate the issue of marital status from financial and parenting issues. A court can bifurcate the proceeding and grant a divorce to end the marital relationship, but leave resolution of other issues to a later time. Bifurcation makes sense when one or both parties want to remarry before other issues are resolved, or when the emotional tension between the parties must be reduced.

## What Is the Legal Significance of a Decree of Divorce?

The decree of divorce is a final judgment entered after a trial or by a stipulation of the parties. In some states, legislation may require a certain time period to elapse after a complaint or petition is filed and served before a decree of divorce or judgment dissolving the marriage is entered. Like other civil judgments, divorce decrees bind both parties to the obligations stated in the decree. Divorce decrees are enforceable by the court.

## What Happens after the Decree of Divorce Is Entered?

Often a decree of divorce will require parties to transfer property, sign documents, separate joint accounts, and work out other details. This takes time and requires cooperation. One party may decide to appeal the final decree or judgment. The time to appeal is limited and specified by law or court rule in each state.

## Is It Possible to Modify a Decree of Divorce?

Parties usually have the right to modify their decree of divorce or final judgment if there is a substantial change in circumstances. Modification proceedings are typically initiated in the same court that entered the final decree or judgment. Modification matters may be litigated or settled.

## Should I Litigate or Settle?

The best way to decide whether to litigate or settle is to weigh the costs of both options. A good attorney can explain to you the merits of litigating versus the merits of settling a contested issue. To determine whether you should litigate, make sure you have considered the cost in time, money, and emotional stress.

Often the cost of settling an issue is significantly less than the financial and emotional cost of litigation. Hundreds of dollars have been spent litigating the ownership of such things as 8-track stereos, old model cars, and avocado-colored appliances. Peace of mind may be more rewarding than fighting it out.

*Settlement proposals should be viewed as an opportunity to open a dialogue.*

## How Should I React to Settlement Proposals?

Your initial reaction to a settlement proposal may be to mistrust it, or even reject it. Try to remember that a settlement proposal is a good faith attempt to resolve the controversy and minimize the associated financial and emotional costs. Consequently, settlement offers should be viewed as an opportunity to open a dialogue. Your spouse's attorney may have some good and creative ideas worthy of your careful consideration. Most family law attorneys recognize that settlements are in everyone's best interest and that relatively few divorce cases actually go to trial.

### *Our Divorce Is Uncontested. Isn't It Better to Let the Attorneys and the Court Handle It?*

Not necessarily. You know more details about your finances and your parenting objectives than does your attorney or the court. You may have more creative ways to resolve the issues.

You might, for example, customize a standard time-sharing schedule to suit your family's unique style and needs. As a rule, standard time-sharing schedules do not make allowances for individual family traditions or unique circumstances. They are imposed only if parents cannot reach their own agreement. Parents always have the opportunity, however, to create a time-sharing arrangement to suit their unique needs.

*13*

# The Legal Issues of Parenting

In law school I had a gifted professor named John Flynn who told his students that the most challenging dilemma we would face in our legal careers would not be a legal question but a moral one.

When I practiced family law, many of my clients would ask me, "How can I win?" As their attorney, I had an ethical duty to zealously advocate their best interests. Consequently, I gathered a formidable bag of tricks to help them "win."

As the years went by, I often agonized over how my aggressive litigation tactics could win legal arguments and coerce settlements in my clients' favor, but at the same time cause emotional and financial havoc to families. I discovered that, despite my gallant efforts as a legal advocate, no one ever really won in a litigated dispute. The thrill of winning was short-lived and, indeed, forgotten by the time my clients began exchanging children for the next weekend or when they received their bill from me.

My most difficult cases were child custody disputes. In my experience, most child custody disputes involved two fit parents fighting for their principles rather than their children's best interest. I saw children, as well as parents, emotionally battered in the process. Even after a custody decision was resolved and one side had "won," it seemed that more had been lost than gained. I concluded that the only time anyone wins in divorce litigation is when the children make it through the process unharmed.

I faced the same moral dilemma as other family law attorneys:

No one ever really "wins" in a litigated dispute. The battle itself creates a lasting bitterness, which is ultimately felt by the children.

how can an attorney zealously fight for a client's parental rights when the very process of fighting usually harms the client, his children, and other family members? None of us wanted to intentionally hurt children during a custody battle. None of us wanted to make our clients' lives even more miserable than they had been before. Yet day after day, we saw the adversarial process inflict pain on innocent parents and children.

Because of a growing awareness of this moral dilemma, the family law bar has been particularly receptive to changes in the family law system—changes that minimize conflict, encourage faster resolution of disputes, and promote co-parenting.

I resolved my moral dilemma by focusing my career on divorce mediation. Mediation provides parents an opportunity to settle their divorce issues in an amicable manner without tearing families apart emotionally.

## Children's Rights

When a divorce first happens, most parents focus on finding out what their rights are. Most parents forget to think about what their children's rights might be. Children have the following rights:

Ongoing bitterness and conflict can be more damaging to the children than the divorce itself.

- Children have the right to have a meaningful relationship with both parents whenever possible.
- Children have the right to remain detached from the strife of their parents' differences.
- Children have the right to love both parents.
- Children have the right to receive love and support from both parents.
- Children have the right to grow up in a physically and emotionally safe environment.
- Children have the right to express their feelings, regardless of their parents' viewpoints.
- Children have the right to be children, free from involvement in the adult world of divorce.

## Reasons Both Parents Need to Maintain a Close Relationship with Their Child

- Aids in a child's healthy emotional development.

- Prepares the child for a change in custody (due to death or serious illness of a custodial parent or a change in the child's needs or requests).

- Prevents a child's distorted or unrealistic fantasies about a parent.

- Alleviates a child's poor self-esteem and guilt (wondering why my other parent does not want to see me).

- Provides gender role modeling by birth parents.

- May prevent power struggles and possible backlash effect between a parent and child.

- May prevent a noncustodial parent from initiating court action.

- May relieve parenting pressures.

- Helps prevent a child from feeling divided loyalties.

- Improves emotional well-being and recovery from divorce for a child and parents.

- Validates importance of birth parents and long-term relationships.

- Provides opportunity for a child's development of an extended family identity.

- Aids in a child's identity development, which is partly maternal and partly paternal.

- Models different parental qualities for a child to learn from.

- Helps maintain parental authority for the child.

- Promotes parental willingness to financially support the child.

- Demonstrates that parents can put aside their personal differences enough to unite regarding their parenting.

Once you determine that you want peace in your life and in your children's lives, it is a matter of committing yourself to this choice. The rest will follow in time.

## Custody

When minor children are involved in a divorce case, a judge

must determine physical and legal custody, as well as financial support. State laws vary on the factors that determine custody of minor children, but generally a court decides custody based on the best interests of the children. The court considers all factors that seem to be relevant, including:

- Which parent is the primary caretaker
- Which custody arrangement keeps siblings together
- The child's relationship with parents, siblings, and any other significant persons
- The relative character and fitness (emotional and physical) of the prospective custodians
- The ability and willingness of each parent to care for the child
- The child's preference, depending on his age and maturity
- The degree of respect each parent has for the parenting rights of the other
- The geographic distance between the parties
- Each parent's willingness and ability to give the other parent access to the child
- Each parent's willingness and ability to cooperate

Generally, a court decides custody based on its perception of the best interests of the children.

Determining the custody of children involves two primary issues: who will make decisions regarding the child, and how will the child's time be shared between both parents. The court gives legal custody to one or both of the parents to make decisions about the health, education, and general welfare of the child. Unless the parents agree upon their own time-sharing schedule, the court will generally impose a standard time-sharing schedule to determine the amount of time each parent will spend with the child. The court will consider circumstances which would necessitate modifying the standard schedule, but these circumstances must be presented to the court.

## Legal Custody (Decision-Making)

Legal custody can be divided into two main categories that

describe the ways in which parents make decisions about their children.

**Sole Legal Custody.** One parent provides a home for the child and is responsible for making all significant legal decisions regarding the child's welfare. The parent with sole legal custody is empowered to make the decisions about medical, dental, and psychological treatment, religious training, and deciding which school the child will attend. It is possible, however, for the noncustodial parent to retain certain decision-making rights and access to records—as long as those rights are specified in the decree of divorce.

In most cases, it is best for the children when both parents are involved in major decisions that affect them.

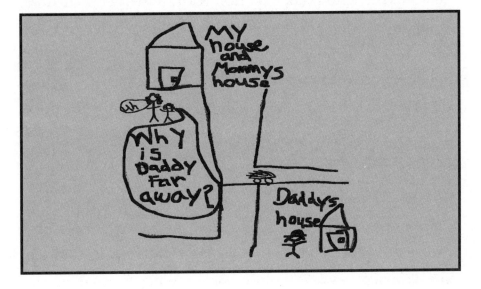

**Joint Legal Custody.** Both parents share decision-making responsibilities regarding the health, education, and general welfare of the child and, whenever possible, consult with each other before making decisions.

Joint legal custody requires a great deal of cooperation on the part of divorcing parents. Many states presume that this arrangement is the most beneficial to the child, but many will allow an order for joint legal custody *only* when both parents formally agree to it. Some courts will order joint legal custody and attempt to force cooperation. The issue of joint custody typically has both strong proponents and opponents.

## Physical Custody (Time-Sharing)

Physical custody refers to the various ways in which parents can share time with a child.

**Sole Physical Custody.** The child resides with, and is supervised by, one parent. The court typically orders a time-sharing schedule with the other parent.

**Joint Physical Custody.** The child resides with both parents and usually spends significant amounts of time with each of them. Joint physical custody does not necessarily mean that a child will spend equal time with both parents. One home may be designated as the primary residence.

**Split Physical Custody.** One child lives primarily with one parent and another child lives with the other parent. Time spent with the noncustodial parent is shared according to a time-sharing plan.

## Parenting Plans

Parenting plans are an emerging trend in the courts today. They place less emphasis on the foregoing legal labels and focus instead on a divorcing couples' own plan for parenting. A parenting plan establishes how parents will make decisions regarding their children, how they will share information, how they will spend time with their children, and how they will resolve other parenting issues. Parents can create a parenting plan on their own, with their attorney, or with a mediator.

# Options to Consider

Every family is unique. You have the opportunity to create a decision-making procedure, time-sharing arrangement, and

> Parenting plans are an emerging trend—allowing parents to design their own plan for parenting.

parenting arrangement that is tailored to your family's needs. As you develop your own plan, you might find the following suggestions helpful.

## Decision-Making Plans for Joint Legal Custody

It is possible to share decision-making powers with your co-parent after your divorce, if you establish a workable procedure and focus on the best interest of your child.

Joint legal custody works best when parents create a plan that describes in detail how shared decision-making will work and includes a tie-breaking procedure. For example, you can agree to gather all relevant information to the subject at issue, brainstorm solutions, and then agree to choose the most sensible decision for everyone involved. If an agreement can't be reached, you might agree to involve a competent third party to assist you in making the final decision.

*Joint legal custody works best when parents design a decision-making procedure.*

Often a plan will empower either parent to make emergency medical decisions when the child is in their physical custody. That parent is then required to notify the other parent.

## Decision-Making Plans for Sole Legal Custody

In a sole legal custody scenario, the sole custodian can still seek the advice and input of the noncustodial parent prior to making a final decision on significant matters involving the child.

A court can award one parent sole legal custody and give the other parent specific parental rights in the decree of divorce. For example, a non-custodial parent can retain the right to be involved in emergency-related decisions, and to access school, medical, dental, and psychological records.

The sole legal custodian should also inform the noncustodial parent of significant events, school activities, illnesses, and other important information regarding the child.

## *Options for Time-Sharing in the Same City*

A receptive mind is needed to create solutions that bring peace. Creativity is within every person, giving rise to solutions previously not seen as possibilities.

- Refer to a standard time-sharing schedule, and modify it according to your family's needs.

- Establish a time and place to get together and plan the monthly calendar. Designate blocks of time for the child to spend with each parent.

- Preview the yearly school calendar, and devise a plan for sharing responsibilities and time with your child.

- For teenagers, in addition to the schedule, designate which parent they need to check in with, and which one will do the chauffeuring when necessary.

- Plan one-on-one time with the child. Each parent can do this with the other parent's cooperation. For example, if there are several children, one parent can spend an evening or a day with one child while the other parent has responsibility for the others.

- Schedule time-sharing with a parent during their day off from work.

- Make a yearly schedule for traditional activities, such as family reunions, school shopping, or holiday parties.

- Alternate time-sharing not only on holidays, but on birthdays, Halloween, school vacations, and other days not covered by a standard time-sharing schedule.

- If you are unable to attend together, take turns attending parent-teacher conferences, back-to-school nights, sports activities, school programs, extracurricular events, recitals, and field trips.

- Modify your time-sharing arrangement when one parent has extra responsibilities, such as work-related training, an extended business trip, or caring for an ill relative.

- Try to arrange your work schedules so that one or the other parent is available to care for the child during evening and bedtime hours.

- Arrange for one parent to care for the children while the other is away on a trip.

- In a custody dispute, agree that the custody evaluator will only decide the primary residence of the children, and that you will negotiate a parenting and time-sharing plan after the evaluation is complete. Such a plan might call for joint legal custody.

- Agree to consider changing the time-sharing arrangement based upon certain specified triggers, such as when a remarriage occurs, or a change in work schedule or employment occurs.

- Become a soccer, basketball, baseball, or softball coach for your child, and join your child on their turf.

- Take karate, tennis, golf, or a community education class with your child.

- Become a community volunteer with your child. Organize and sponsor a neighborhood service project—visiting a nursing home or cleaning up the community—with your child and their friends.

- Volunteer in your child's classroom. Participate in class parties.

- Write letters and notes to your child. Be creative. Send funny jokes and riddles that make your child laugh; send a love note that makes your child feel important; or write something special that maintains the connection between you and your child.

- Leave fun phone messages for your child.

### Options for Long Distance Time-Sharing

- Divide the summer vacation or the blocks of time provided in a year-round school calendar between parents. Use vacations for a special trip or one-on-one time with the child.

- Agree that the out-of-town parent will come to see the child regularly, either according to a schedule or as negotiated.

- When finances permit, consider having the child travel to see the out-of-town parent.

- Establish a telephone schedule. For example, the absent parent might call the child at the same time on the same day every week, or more frequently when possible.

- Exchange video or audio tapes featuring the absent parent reading or telling stories, updating the child about personal events, and expressing love for the child.

- Send the absent parent duplicate video tapes or photographs of significant events or moments in the child's life.

- Include time with grandparents as a means of connecting with the extended family of the absent parent. Arrange for the grandparents to include the children in family celebrations and reunions.

- If you are the out-of-town parent, give your child self-addressed, stamped envelopes so that your child can write you letters or send you drawings and other surprises, whenever they choose.

- Send letters frequently to your child and send surprises in the mail, such as autumn leaves, interesting news articles about your community, and other momentos.

## Child Support

### What Is Child Support?

*Children should not be brought into discussions about family finances.*

If there are minor children involved in a divorce action, the court will enter an order for their financial support. Typically one parent is ordered to pay a monthly child support payment to the other parent who is the primary caretaker to help them provide for the financial needs of the children.

Because the general welfare of minor children is of paramount concern, the court will order the payment of child support. Child support is generally viewed as a vested right of a minor child. Consequently, no parent can waive a child's right to receive financial support. Most child support laws recognize that parents have a joint responsibility to provide for the financial needs of their children.

Child support that is paid to one parent is intended to help that parent meet the basic needs of a child for food, shelter, clothing, routine medical and dental treatment, and education. Often state laws require parents to share any uninsured medical, dental, and psychological expenses of a minor child.

The court will order the payment of child support until a child reaches the age of majority, which is usually eighteen years of age. The court may order support past that age when a child is physically or mentally handicapped, or when other special circumstances exist.

Under federal tax law, child support is not considered taxable income to the recipient parent and is not allowed as a deduction for the payor parent. Check with your accountant to find out more about the tax consequences of child support in your state.

## How Is the Amount of Child Support Determined?

The amount of support is determined by considering the financial circumstances of both parents and the relative needs of the minor children involved.

All states have enacted guidelines for determining the amount of child support, based on the physical custody arrangement of the child. Generally, the guidelines use a formula based on the parents' gross income and a corresponding table to determine the amount of support required on a per-child basis. State statutes

All states have enacted guidelines for determining the amount of child support.

usually permit deviating from the guidelines in special circumstances.

Some courts rely completely on child support guidelines, while others use the guidelines only as a reference tool. The court may hold a hearing to consider all relevant evidence and determine the appropriate amount of support. Then the court will order payment.

This court-ordered support continues even if the child resides in another state. The court reserves the power to modify the amount and payment terms if a significant change of circumstances occurs. It also reserves the power to enforce the payment of child support.

If a parent fails to pay child support, they may face contempt proceedings. These typically result in wage garnishment, community service hours, the imposition of a judgment, or even, in rare circumstances, jail time.

## Suggestions Regarding Child Support:

- Choose your time-sharing arrangement first. Then use the child support guidelines and any worksheets that relate to your physical custody arrangements, as provided by your state, to help determine the appropriate amount of support for your child.

- Rather than argue in court about the amount of child support, look at all the factors the judge will have to consider, and make your own objective determination of your child's needs.

- Devise an equitable formula for sharing uninsured medical, dental, and psychological expenses incurred by a minor child. This allocation may be 50-50, or it may be based on the relative income of each parent.

- Set up bank or trust accounts, or make other investments, to cover future expenses, such as school fees, a car, orthodontic treatments, or emergencies.

- If you are the parent receiving child support, describe to the other parent what expenses the child support will pay. Disclosing the amount needed to pay utilities, food, clothing, educational expenses, rent or mortgage, and other child-raising expenses usually prevents the payor parent from feeling resentful.

- Because child support usually ends when a minor child reaches the age of majority, agree that you will extend it until the child graduates from high school. You might even agree to continue it through college.

- Agree that, after they reach the age of majority, the child will be responsible for their own expenses and will discuss financial assistance with each parent.

- Invest in life insurance policies for the benefit of minor children in the event of a parental death.

- Consider sharing other child-rearing expenses that go above and beyond basic needs, such as extracurricular school expenses, car insurance, uniforms, presents, and summer camps.

- Devise an equitable formula for sharing the cost of extracurricular activities, such as sports, music lessons, karate, theater, and church-sponsored activities. This may be a 50-50 split, or it may be proportionate to each parent's income. You might also agree that one parent will sponsor a particular sport or extracurricular activity and pay all expenses.

## A Judge's Perspective

The following excerpt was taken from an interview by Elizabeth Hickey with Judge Michael Murphy, the presiding judge of the Third District Court in Salt Lake City, Utah.

E. Hickey: What is the guiding principle that a judge will use when making decisions regarding the children?

Judge Murphy: The Appeals Court tells us that we must look at what is in the best interest of the children. That can mean a lot of things, such as which parent is going to assist the other parent in getting lots of time-sharing. We look for what is going to help the kids.

E. Hickey: Sometimes the words that are used in the legal system and the courts are confusing to a child and may carry unintended messages. What do you think about that?

Judge Murphy: I have been trying to take out of my vocabulary words that could cause children to feel like pieces of property, such as "deliver the children here or there," when discussing time-sharing issues. I have to admit that the words the court, judges, lawyers, and parents use are not the best words. They are bad habits that, hopefully, we can break. In changing our words and substance, we can hope to change our sensitivities.

E. Hickey: The term "visitation" is often used in court language. When the courts use that term, what do they really mean?

Judge Murphy: Time with a child is much more than a visit. It is going to the other parent's home and being with that parent. The "visit" doesn't mean visiting to the child. Visitation does not mean that it's a superficial relationship. When we have "visitation problems" we often see logistical problems involving time and travel. One thing I try to do is to make sure that the parent who does not have the child during the school year has extensive rights during the summer months.

E. Hickey: When dealing with custody or visitation issues, how attentive do you think most judges are?

Judge Murphy: In cases where children are involved, the judge's interest is heightened. We are not just talking about the car, the house, or the dog. When it comes to children, we are talking about flesh and blood, rather than assets. So, while our language may not always be the most sensitive, the hearts of judges are really in the right place.

E. Hickey: What types of visitation problems do you hear about in the courtroom?

Judge Murphy: We have problems when a child doesn't get to see one parent. We also see problems when a child does not want to spend time with the other parent. Sometimes the child has legitimate reasons, such as that they don't want to be away from their friends or their activities. As a result, they don't have as much time with the other parent as that parent would like.

In a divorce, both parents must sacrifice, and the sad thing is that the children might have to do the same thing. They might have to sacrifice material things, or as much time with their friends as they would like, or other activities, in order to maintain this relationship with the other parent.

E. Hickey: Can you give us an example of what happens when parents come to court and request joint custody?

Judge Murphy: I had a case today where both parents came in. The father was asking for joint legal custody, with his home being designated as the primary residence. I asked them a few questions, such as, "How long have you been separated?" and "How has the joint custody arrangement worked so far?"

If there are any problems raised at this point, I ask a few more questions. In this case, the mother asked, "If he doesn't like the way I do certain things, can he stop me from having visitation?"

I asked, "What do you mean? Are there big problems?" She answered, "He doesn't like the way I got our son's hair cut." After inquiring about the haircut, I told her that the father could not condition visiting rights on "doing things his way."

E. Hickey: What do courts generally think about joint custody arrangements for children?

Judge Murphy: I think the courts will generally do anything they can to make it easier for both parents to be actively involved in a healthy way in their child's life. I do everything I can to facilitate the relationship between the parents and the kids.

There are circumstances where parents ask for joint custody out of pride. But in the vast majority of cases, it comes down to the best interests of the child. Most parents will seek joint custody because they have the child's best interest in mind, and they really want to participate in and be a part of the child's life. They want to participate in parent-teacher conferences and get a copy of the child's report card.

E. Hickey: Does our current adversarial court system set parents up to compete with each other?

Judge Murphy: One of the worst things courts do is help foster the concept of winners and losers. There's a plaintiff against a defendant. One is awarded alimony, child support, and custody. The other is awarded visitation.

It is unfortunate, but it is language that we use in other areas of the law. It is not intended to demean a winner or loser. In fact, if it is a contested case, everyone will be a loser. If the language somehow makes people feel they must win, then we should change the language.

What is important is to change the mind-set that the language creates. People need to do things to work out their hostilities: jog, ski, say something to your mother-in-law. Work things out in a way that shows your children are the winners. If your motivation is only for rewards, then it is the children you'll be hurting.

If you can attempt to perceive every situation from the perspective of "How will this affect my child?" then you will be farther ahead in the long run. I think your children will benefit greatly, and there will be satisfaction from doing what is best for the children.

E. Hickey: Does the court have concern for children's feelings? When parents split up, children often express that they, too, feel like they are divorcing a parent.

Judge Murphy: When a divorce occurs, it is important that the divorce is between the parents, and not the parents and children. If it is a circumstance where only one parent will have formal custody of the children, I look for, among other factors, which parent is most willing to foster a growing and supportive relationship with the other parent.

The parent who gives me the best impression of supporting the children's relationship with the other parent is going to have a step up in winning custody. A parent who supports and encourages a child's relationship with the other parent is almost always acting in the best interests of the child.

E. Hickey: So many children wonder if the divorce between their parents had something to do with them. They wonder if they could have been the cause of their parents' problems. What do you think about that?

Judge Murphy: I don't know of any case where the child has been the cause of divorce. Divorces occur between people because there is bad chemistry between the people; because they have arguments over money, religion, life. There may have been arguments over the children, but that is an excuse.

E. Hickey: Often children who do not see their noncustodial parent on a regular basis assume that the parent is not interested in them or has rejected them. What do you say to these children?

Judge Murphy: It is difficult for me to tell a child how to handle something. It is difficult to say that if someone treats you like that they are not worth your time, because that is the child's mother or father. That parent is important to the child.

Children wonder about their parents and want to know who their parents are. Parents are supposed to be the mature ones. They are supposed to know what their obligations are. But parenting is much more than an obligation. A parent should be someone you really love. Sometimes a parent who has "abandoned the picture" hasn't really grown up. Maybe they are still immature. A child who can understand this is much more grown-up than the parent.

E. Hickey: We know from several studies that many divorced parents say unkind things about the other parent to the child. What do you think of this?

Judge Murphy: When the separation occurs, there is a lot of pain and hostility. A parent may say something hurtful that a child overhears. A child is made up of both parents' chromosomes, and they are dramatically affected when they hear one parent say something bad about the other parent.

In most cases it is unintentional, but you have to presume that the child can read your body language and is able to feel the anger you might be feeling. You can just imagine how the child might react to that. This is why parents need to take the steps necessary to resolve the anger they are feeling, so they can move forward.

I think children will think less of the verbally condescending parent than of the other parent. Parents should do whatever they can to reduce the possibility of saying mean things to a child about the child's other parent.

*In regards to my behavior, I can only plead insanity . . . because ever since my children were born, the moment I looked at them, I was crazy about them. Once I held them, I was hooked. I'm addicted to my children, sir.*

*I love them with all my heart and the idea of someone telling me I can't be with them, I can't see them every day, it's like someone saying I can't have air. I can't live without air and I can't live without them.*

*Listen, I would do anything, I just want to be with them, you know that I need that, sir. We have a history. And I just . . . they mean everything to me and they need me as much as I need them. So please, don't take my kids away from me.*

*Thank you.*

—Daniel, pleading with the judge
from the movie *Mrs. Doubtfire*

# 14
## *The Mechanics of Co-parenting*

One doesn't discover new lands without consenting to lose sight of the shore for a very long time.
—André Gide

When a divorce occurs, a family breaks apart. The deep wound of divorce causes pain in the hearts of each family member, including extended family members. Unless the wound is healed, broken hearts can stay broken for years, even from generation to generation.

In order to heal the wound of a family split apart, the family must mend itself. From the shattered dreams and fragments of a former life torn apart by marital strife, parents can rebuild a new family. From one home can emerge two homes. Parents can mold the foundation of a healed family from the dust of a dysfunctional family system. In the restructured family, peace, love, and forgiveness can replace conflict and pain.

The decision to restructure your family after divorce is an act of healing. Although mediators, counselors, attorneys, and other advisers can help you rebuild your new family, the decision to become a co-parent must come from within your heart. When the decision is made to let go of the pain and work toward mending your family, the healing begins.

Although your divorce will end your marital relationship, your relationship as parents will continue forever. You and your former spouse have the opportunity to make that relationship positive and constructive rather than negative and destructive. The choice is yours.

Creating a co-parenting relationship with a former spouse is not easy, but by taking one step at a time it is possible. As you succeed in building a co-parenting relationship, you will see immediate results in the lives of your children. As you reduce conflict and encourage communication, your children will feel more secure and less afraid.

The secret to successful co-parenting is putting the needs of your children ahead of your own. When both parents focus on the needs and interests of the children, an effective co-parenting relationship miraculously emerges. Learn how to separate your needs from your child's, and when interacting with your co-parent, focus specifically on your child's needs.

# Steps to Successful Co-parenting

## 1. Be Committed

The first step in establishing a co-parenting relationship is simply making the commitment to foster successful parenting for your child despite the divorce. This decision must include a conviction to begin acting unselfishly, maturely, and reasonably with your former spouse.

In many situations, one parent is more committed to co-parenting than the other. Most parents intend to be good parents. However, unresolved feelings of anger, sadness, disappointment, and hurt often prevent a parent from cooperating as a co-parent.

Initially, I was more committed to co-parenting than my former spouse was. It took several months for him to trust that we could raise our two daughters in a cooperative manner despite the divorce. When he caught the vision that being reasonable and cooperative with me benefited our children, he adopted this approach wholeheartedly. My former husband and I now trade favors, sit next to each other at school programs, and recently set up savings accounts for our children's college educations.

If you show your former spouse that you are committed to being a cooperative co-parent, your choice may influence his/her to make a similar choice. This has been my own experience, and I see it happen time after time to the clients in my mediation practice.

## 2. Create a Vision

The second step is to visualize how you would like your new co-parenting relationship to look, and to share that vision with your co-parent. Parents *can* redesign their family during a divorce. Adopt the perspective that only the marriage relationship is ending; the parent-child relationship will continue forever.

The image of a restructured family must include the idea that there are positives that can happen as one home turns into two. You can focus on the abundance of new possibilities, rather than on the loss of a traditional family life. Co-parenting can revitalize the parent-child relationship by motivating more one-on-one time.

With the creation of two homes, a remarriage may bring the opportunity of new relationships with stepparents and stepsiblings. Families grow and these additions give children more people to love and support them.

People are always blaming their circumstances for what they are. I don't believe in circumstances. The people who get on in this world are the people who get up and look for the circumstances they want, and, if they can't find them, make them.
—George
Bernard Shaw

The vision of a successful co-parenting relationship includes behaving in the same ways you would have your co-parent behave towards you. Each of you has the responsibility to heal your own anger, disappointment, and grief about the divorce as quickly as possible, to avoid burdening your child. In addition, each of you will benefit from being proactive in cooperating with the other parent.

Co-parenting requires both parents to set aside personal differences and cooperate maturely and respectfully. The greatest test of your maturity occurs in a co-parenting relationship. Maturity is the ability to be assertive rather than aggressive; constructive rather than destructive; forgiving rather than resentful; open-minded rather than closed-minded; reasonable rather than stubborn. There is no greater opportunity for your child to learn maturity than from seeing a successful co-parenting relationship.

It is useful to visualize a co-parenting relationship as a business relationship. Co-parenting is essentially a partnership or joint venture with the objective of raising successful and well-adjusted children. Effective business partners work together and focus on common goals and objectives. Your success will result from setting up good communication channels, respecting strengths as well as limitations, brainstorming ideas, and making sensible decisions.

*Human relationships require a willingness to accept other people as they are, and not for what we want them to be.*

### 3. Do It

The third step in successful co-parenting is simply doing it. The adage "practice makes perfect" fits. Successful co-parenting means working daily to make your vision a reality.

Co-parenting requires a determined commitment to the vision of a parenting plan to benefit your child. Each obstacle can be overcome if both of you have a willingness to start over and try different approaches, until you find out what works best for all of you.

*Do or do not. There is no try.*
*—Yoda*

By taking cooperative and reasonable approaches toward problem solving, you will be able to work out compromises without "giving in."

Co-parenting is building on what *is* working in your new relationship rather than what did not work in the past. It is about seeing your former spouse as a resource rather than as an enemy. As co-parents you trade favors and focus your attention on your child.

Co-parenting depends on setting up new emotional boundaries and allowing your child to have his own emotions, identity, and choices. It requires leaving the past in the past, and focusing on the present and the future. Most importantly, it requires never forgetting the vision that you are working together for your child's greatest benefit.

## Divorce Mediation

Litigation         vs.         Mediation

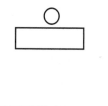
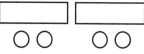
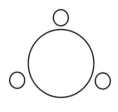

### What Is Mediation?

Mediation is a voluntary settlement process that gives a divorcing couple the opportunity to sit together at the bargaining table to design a settlement with the assistance of a neutral intermediary. In most cases, the attorneys representing the parents are not present. A mediator acts as a specially trained facilitator to help the co-parents make practical, informed decisions to resolve their parenting issues. The mediator's recommendations are equitable and are presented in a win-win manner.

Mediation works within the adversarial legal system without depriving the parties of the protections afforded by the legal process. It supplements the legal process by achieving better results for the parties and their children. After agreements are reached in mediation, they are then reviewed by the parties' attorneys and formalized in a decree of divorce or modification order.

Mediation is not counseling. A mediator helps the parties put aside their emotional issues and focus on making sensible decisions based on facts. A mediator will not give legal advice and cannot make decisions for the parties. Instead, the mediator will help the parties negotiate their own settlements.

## When Is Mediation Successful?

Mediation is successful if both spouses are willing to put aside their emotional differences and focus on settlement options that make the most sense under the circumstances and allow everyone to win, especially the children. Mediation is especially helpful for parents desiring to create a parenting plan.

## Why Mediate?

The stress of resolving divorce issues can be intense. Mediation gives parents the opportunity to leave the battleground and sit together at the bargaining table. On an equal playing field, using the services of an impartial referee, parents are in a better position to settle issues in a fair and objective manner.

Mediation affords parties the opportunity to resolve parenting and financial issues by sitting face to face instead of communicating through attorneys or waiting for a judge to make a decision. Consequently it is an efficient problem-solving process and is more economical than resolving an issue through litigation.

Mediation shifts the focus from past marital problems to resolution of present and future issues in a constructive and

Research shows that parents are much more likely to honor their own parenting agreements reached through mediation.

positive manner. Typically, agreements reached through mediation are long-lasting, because parents have made their own resolutions.

### How Long Does Mediation Take?

As a rule, it takes four hours (two mediation sessions) to resolve parenting issues. Resolving financial issues may take four to six hours. If the issues are complex, or if emotional impasses arise, mediation may take longer.

### How Much Does It Cost?

Generally, fees are based on hourly rates, set by the mediator or the court. The fees are usually shared equally by the parties.

### Must All Issues Be Mediated?

No. You can decide to mediate certain issues and have your attorney or a judge resolve other issues.

### Will I Still Need a Lawyer?

Yes. Mediation is not a substitute for legal advice. Your lawyer is your adviser on the law. A good mediator will require you to seek legal advice during the mediation process.

### What Are the Benefits of Mediation?

- You and your parenting partner can self-determine what is best for your family.
- Mediation can be less costly than litigation.
- Mediation is private and confidential. Because all discussions are privileged settlement negotiations, the parties cannot testify about what was said during mediation.
- Meetings are scheduled at the convenience of the parties.
- Mediation gives parents the opportunity to learn to cooperate for the benefit of their children and sets the stage for cooperative post-divorce interactions.
- Mediators are informed about divorce issues and can inform parents of all necessary information to make sensible decisions.

> Resolutions fashioned by the parties in mediation are better suited for them than those negotiated by attorneys or imposed by the court.

- Resolutions fashioned by parents through a mediation session are often more creative and better suited to a family's needs than solutions negotiated by attorneys or imposed by a court.

- Mediation encourages parents to cooperate, rather than fight, to resolve issues.

- Parents learn new and better skills to communicate and solve problems through mediation.

- A final settlement can usually be reached more quickly than with other alternatives. Because both parties make a personal investment in the settlement, it is less likely that either one will return to court for a modification.

*The very act of choosing to mediate sets up an environment of hope that your differences can be settled.*

## Who Should Act as a Mediator?

Competent mediators should have a professional background in law, social work, mental health, or education and be specially trained in mediation and negotiation techniques. From an ethical standpoint, a mediator should be a disinterested party who has had no previous relationship with the couple or either party, particularly in the capacity of an attorney or therapist. In most states, an attorney-mediator cannot act as a mediator and also represent one or both of the parties as an attorney before the court.

*Choosing mediation demonstrates to your children that personal conflicts can be worked through.*

## What Should I Look for in a Mediator?

The best mediators are those who have a background in both family law and counseling. Divorce is a legal process and so the mediator must be knowledgeable in family law issues. The dissolution of a marriage can sometimes resemble the dissolution of a complex business, so it helps if the mediator has a knowledge of business, real estate, and accounting too. Competent mediators usually have an accessible network of experts who can assist in valuing and dividing assets, and rendering advice on taxes and other specialized matters.

Moreover, a mediator must have basic counseling skills, to not only assist couples in putting aside the emotional issues, but to identify the therapeutic interventions that may be appropriate to provide emotional support to a family. In addition, a good mediator will be able to identify when a person is not emotionally able to make rational and fair agreements.

A well-qualified divorce mediator will have at least forty hours of training from a program approved by the Academy of Family Mediators, which is the largest nationally recognized professional organization of family mediators. Your safest bet for a family mediator is a lawyer or therapist who has specialized in divorce mediation.

## How Can I Encourage My Spouse to Try Mediation?

*For mediation to be successful both partners must be committed to the process.*

If there is a high level of mistrust, one spouse may immediately reject the other spouse's request for mediation. That spouse may mistakenly believe that mediation will somehow be more favorable to the other spouse.

Mediation is a process that does not favor one spouse over the other. Mediation seeks win-win solutions. However, for mediation to be successful, both parties must be committed to the process.

If there still exists some trust in your relationship, try explaining to your spouse the benefits of mediation for both of you and for your children. Emphasize the time and cost efficiency of mediation compared to the lengthy and expensive process of divorce litigation. Explain the emotional benefits of mediation for your spouse as well as for your children.

Invite your spouse to interview and help choose a trained mediator. Share success stories of friends and family members who have used a mediator to help settle issues. Most importantly, point out that mediation offers an opportunity for you and your spouse to be an example to your children of how to resolve conflicts in a positive way.

If there exists a high level of mistrust in your relationship, ask your attorney to suggest mediation to your spouse's attorney. Most family law attorneys are aware of the benefits of mediation, especially when children are involved. If that effort fails, petition the court for an order requiring your spouse to try mediation. A judge who is concerned about lessening his or her work load or minimizing the conflict and expense will eagerly refer your case to a qualified mediator.

*Remember, when both sides feel they have been treated fairly, the road to peace has been well paved.*

Even if your spouse refuses to try mediation now, never give up. Down the road, after emotions subside and legal bills accumulate, mediation may look more appealing to your spouse.

## Success Stories of Mediation

As a court-appointed mediator in child custody disputes, I receive some of the courts' most difficult cases. Typically, the court only orders cases to mediation if communication between the two parties has deteriorated severely. Therefore, I assume that most of the cases I am assigned will have difficulty reaching resolution. Despite my assumptions, my clients have surprised me in amazing ways.

My clients have taught me that it doesn't matter how difficult the issues are or how many problems existed in the past. If two parents have the desire to start over and make co-parenting work for the benefit of their children, miracles can happen.

In each my mediation cases, I take parents away from the adversarial environment of a lawyer's office or a courtroom and invite them into my home. Rather than being a detriment, my home has afforded divorcing parents with a peaceful setting to resolve family issues. Through the mediation process, many of my clients have found a place in their hearts for peace and healing.

The following are summaries of cases where I expected mediation to fail. Nevertheless, these parents successfully created a parenting plan because of their commitment to co-parenting.

### Case One—Bill and Kathy

I was certain mediation would not work in the case of Bill and Kathy. Bill had been recently extradited to Utah from Florida, where he had been arrested for kidnapping their three children. The children were returned to Kathy, who was awarded immediate temporary custody.

Kathy and Bill had not spoken to each other for six years. During those six years, they had lived with intense feelings of anger, betrayal, and distrust. Sitting at my dining room table, I gave them an opportunity to talk about their children.

As they talked, they put aside their anger and focused on the common love they shared for each child. Bill accepted responsibility for his mistake in taking the children away. Kathy listened to Bill's acknowledgement of this hurtful judgment call. With her heart softened, she shared how she now felt like a stranger to their three children. Two of the children wanted to go back with their father, but one was willing to stay with Kathy for a while longer.

Bill acknowledged that he had made negative comments about Kathy and could see the loyalty conflict that had emerged. Kathy admitted that she could not begin relationships with their three children unless she had Bill's support in repairing the relationships. They both felt financially burdened with attorney's fees and were emotionally exhausted from courtroom show-downs. They decided to start over.

Once Kathy and Bill had made that commitment, the rest was easy. They agreed to meet with their children at a park and

> If your spouse refuses to go to mediation, never give up. Mediation may look more appealing to your spouse down the road.

explain their vision of cooperative parenting. Their children would have the chance to have two parents in their lives again, parents who cared about them and shared time with them. There would no longer be a need for divided loyalties.

Bill pledged his support in reversing the brainwashing that had been done. Kathy agreed to allow two of the children to have primary residence with Bill, planning to rebuild her relationship with them one step at a time.

## Case Two—Rob and Denise

Rob and Denise reluctantly entered mediation after being referred to me by the court. They were arguing over the custody of four children. Prior to their mediation, I learned from their attorneys that Denise had been hospitalized for several months during the marriage for depression caused by severe childhood sexual abuse. Rob had assumed the primary caretaker role for the children. Based on my experience as a divorce attorney, I knew that Rob had an excellent chance of having the court award him sole custody of the children.

During the first few minutes of their mediation session, each parent expressed their deep concern for the well-being of their children and their recognition of the importance of having their children spend quality time with each of them.

Denise expressed her desire to finish her personal healing process and start over in her mothering role. Rob confessed that because his job was so demanding, he would have difficulty assuming sole custody of the children.

After putting aside their adversarial agendas, they started working together in designing a time-sharing arrangement that met the needs of all four children. Rob and Denise agreed on a joint custody arrangement and created a detailed parenting plan.

## Case Three—Jose and Maria

Jose and Maria came to mediation extremely distrustful of one another. Jose was worried that Maria would take their two sons and return to their former home in Mexico. Jose was settled in the United States and had filed for custody and an injunction preventing Maria from taking the children out of the state.

Neither Jose or Maria had communicated directly with one another since their separation. Their attorneys were their sole means of communication. Mediation gave them an opportunity to talk to each other face to face.

During the mediation session, Jose talked about his fear of Maria taking the children to Mexico and about the deep feelings of loss he would experience if that occurred. Maria shared her feelings of loneliness and her desire to live with her family in Mexico. She was also worried about financial security.

As I focused the discussion on the needs of their two boys, both parents shifted their perspective. They realized that there were many solutions to their dilemma. Maria saw that the boys needed to have their father in their lives as a role model and companion. She started looking at ways she could improve her job skills. Jose recognized that he could lessen the financial burdens on Maria if he sacrificed and provided more financial resources to her. Once he agreed to do so, she gave up her plans to return to Mexico. With this beginning, they designed a cooperative co-parenting plan.

These three difficult cases succeeded because each parent was willing to be committed to a co-parenting vision. Despite challenging circumstances, these parents focused on the needs of the children and decided to meet *their children's needs* ahead of personal agendas. In addition, these parents listened to each other and through understanding the other's perspective, were able to work more constructively as co-parents to find win-win solutions.

## Parenting Plans

Successful co-parenting is not a usual by-product of most adversarial divorces. Most parents have no idea what shared parenting requires. Most post-divorce conflicts arise because of misunderstandings and poor communication. Conflict can be prevented by making a parenting plan.

After you decide to create a co-parenting relationship, you may appreciate some guidance in creating a parenting plan. A mediator can assist in this process as well as in settling other issues of divorce. Using the detailed worksheets and examples of a parenting plan provided in this chapter, you can design your own co-parenting arrangement.

Many states are encouraging parents to negotiate a parenting plan during the divorce process. A parenting plan provides guidelines for:

- How parents will make decisions regarding their children
- How they will share information
- How they will spend time with their children
- Ways to resolve other parenting issues

None of us is smarter than all of us.
—Satchel Paige

# *Parenting Plan Worksheet*

1. Desired goals of co-parenting:
   a.

   b.

   c.

2. Communication ground rules:
   a.

   b.

   c.

   d.

   e.

3. Time-sharing arrangement: (list all options)
   a. Monthly schedule (refer to calendar, if helpful)

   b. Vacation times

   c. Holidays

   d. Special days (birthdays, parents' birthdays)

   e. Special occasions (weddings, funerals, graduations)

   f. School, sports, church and community events (back–to-school night, parent-teacher conferences, school programs, sports events, church programs)

   g. Grandparent time-sharing arrangements

4. Transportation details:
   a. Transportation responsibilities, exchange times and places

   b. Special instructions or restrictions

5. Telephone schedule:
   a. When children are with Mom

   b. When children are with Dad

6. Long-distance parenting arrangement:
   (If one parent lives more than 100 miles away)
   a. Yearly time-sharing schedule

   b. Transportation details (including allocation of transportation costs)

   c. Logistics of sharing information

7. Procedure for making decisions:
   a. How should major decisions be made and by whom?
      (education, daycare, medical and dental treatment, therapy)

   b. If you desire to share the decision-making responsibility, how will disagreements be resolved? Devise tie-breaking procedures.

8. Procedure for sharing information:
   a. School-related information (report cards, academic or disciplinary problems, parent-teacher conferences, school activities)

   b. Extracurricular activities

   c. Health-related information (illnesses, prescriptions, checkups, therapy sessions, etc.)

   d. Community and special events

9. Agenda for a parenting meeting: (on a monthly or weekly basis)
   a.

   b.

   c.

10. Child support:
    a. Amount (determined by applicable worksheet)

b. Should child support be recalculated in the future? If so, when and how?

c. Payment schedule

d. Payment of child care expenses:

    i. By whom

    ii. Verification

    iii. Procedure to follow if child care expenses change

e. Itemization of what child support covers and procedure for paying extraordinary child-related expenses, if agreed upon

f. Percentage allocation of medical/dental/psychological expenses not paid by insurance

11. Health insurance:
    a. Carried by whom

    b. Procedure for changing insurance coverage

    c. Claims procedure

12. Post-high school education for children:
    a. Any minimum guarantees to children

    b. Contributions by parents and/or financial planning options

    c. Financial planning options

The following is an example of a parenting agreement.

## *Parenting Agreement*

We,_____ and _____, through the assistance of a mediator, have reached an agreement regarding certain parenting issues for the benefit of our children, on this _____ day of _____, 19___ .

In making this Agreement, we acknowledge the following:

A. We have chosen to resolve our parenting issues through the process of mediation because we feel confident in our abilities to problem-solve with each other as parents in a reasonable and fair manner.

B. We are both dedicated parents who, although divorced, desire to create a co-parenting relationship for the benefit of our children.

C. We recognize that we may have made mistakes in the past and desire to start over as better, more committed parents.

D. We agree to focus on the needs and interests of our children ahead of our own. We desire to give our children the opportunity to have a meaningful relationship with both of us.

E. Any specific time-sharing schedule must focus upon meeting our children's emotional needs, as much as possible. Because these needs will change over time, we agree to approach establishing and revising a time-sharing schedule in a flexible manner as set forth below.

F. We agree to establish and maintain good communication with each other and to establish a cooperative working relationship as parents.

G. Because of our common concern for our children's emotional well-being, we enter into this Agreement.

Based on these premises, we agree that the following rules will govern our relationship:

### *Ground Rules*

1. We agree that our working relationship as parents shall be built on trust and cooperation.

2. We agree to trade favors frequently. This will encourage cooperation and flexibility in our parenting relationship and prevent resentments from accumulating between us.

3. We believe open, honest, and direct communication between us is essential to an effective parenting relationship. We agree to take affirmative steps to adapt procedures, ensuring that we have frequent communication in a civil manner.

4. We agree to support each other in our respective parenting roles. We recognize that we may have different parenting styles from time to time.

5. We agree to affirmatively support each other as parents by giving compliments to each other, giving our children permission to love both parents, and by showing appreciation for favors given.

6. We agree that spending quality time with the children is most important, and we agree to cooperate with each other and adjust our time-sharing arrangement to ensure that this is possible.

7. We recognize that conflict between us causes emotional trauma and pain to the children. We agree to be civil to one another in all of our future dealings.

8. We recognize that it is important for our children's emotional well-being that we hold the other parent in high esteem as a parent in our respective conversations with the children throughout their lives.

9. We agree to leave the past in the past. We agree to start today working together as co-parents and seeing the other parent as a resource.

## Parenting Meeting

We agree to meet the first_____of each month/week or have a telephone conversation to discuss our time-sharing arrangement for the month/week and to share information regarding our children. We agree to reschedule this meeting within a reasonable time if that day is inconvenient for one of us.

## Time-Sharing Schedule

We agree to prepare a monthly calendar so that our time-sharing schedule may be summarized, in writing, from month to month. We agree to review the time-sharing options and to formulate a schedule that will be in the best interest of our children. We agree to be flexible with each other if minor changes are necessary. We agree that the following schedule should be our guide:

**1. Definition of "block time."** We agree to spend blocks of time with each child. Each block of time will be ____days in length and will begin at 6:00 P.M. and continue until 6:00 P.M. on the designated return date. Our children will go to the other parent's home together. However,_____will return to _____'s home one day earlier than _____ in order to enable_____ to have some one-on-one time with _____ and to allow_____ to have one-on-one time with_____.

The parent picking up the children is responsible for the children's dinner.

**2. Birthdays.** For the children's birthdays, we agree that whoever has the children during their "block period" will have the child's birthday party. We agree that the parent who is "off block" is free to plan a party the day before or the day after the child's birthday. We agree to work together to make birthdays special for our children.

**3. Vacation.** We agree to discuss with each other how we want to spend our respective vacation time with the children. We will work out an arrangement that is mutually acceptable to both of us. We do agree, however, to give advance notice to the other parent of a planned vacation. If possible, we agree to give two weeks notice.

**4. Holidays.** We agree to spend time with our children on holidays as per the court's standard time-sharing schedule.

**5. Babysitter rule.** We agree to call the other parent, whenever possible, for our babysitting needs.

**6. Revision of time-sharing schedule.** In order to better meet the emotional needs of our children, we agree to revise the time-sharing schedule, if necessary, by consulting with one another and cooperatively establishing a new time-sharing schedule. We also agree to consider revising our schedule if a significant change occurs in either of our lives. We agree to first meet with each other to modify the time-sharing arrangement as set forth above. Then, if we are unable to agree upon a new time-sharing schedule, we agree to hire a mediator to assist us before we seek a resolution in court.

## Sharing Information

1. We agree to use our best efforts to communicate and share information with each other on a frequent basis regarding our children's development, school work, medical and dental treatment, therapy, and regarding other information appropriate to share with the other parent.

2. We agree to affirmatively notify the other parent of all school programs, church events, extracurricular activities, and sporting events that involve one or more of our children.

3. We agree to notify the other parent of significant illnesses the children may have when they are at our individual homes.

4. We agree to discuss any problems either of us is experiencing with disciplining our children.

5. We agree to immediately advise the other parent of any changes in our address, telephone number, or other information pertinent to communication.

6. We agree to advise the other parent of all logistical details regarding vacation time with our children, including places and telephone numbers where the children may be reached.

7. We both agree that we will communicate with each other both by telephone and in person. We agree that it is important for our children to see us working together in a positive and constructive way.

## Consistency in Discipline and Parenting

1. We agree that consistency is one of the key elements in raising children. Therefore, we would like to see the same curfews and bedtimes implemented at each of our homes.

2. We recognize that our discipline and parenting of our children will be more effective if we work as a "united front." Therefore, we agree to discuss discipline and philosophies with each other and come to a consensus as to what works.

## Major Decisions

1. **Decision-making procedure.** We agree that all major decisions concerning our children, including their health, education, and general welfare, daycare, education, medical and dental treatment, and therapy will be discussed. Further, we agree to use the following decision-making procedure:

   a. Identify the issue

   b. Brainstorm possible solutions

   c. Choose the most sensible solution that considers the needs and interests of everyone involved

2. **Tie-breaking procedure.** We agree to meet and discuss major decisions together, focusing on objective criteria and facts, and involving any professionals who may be of

assistance. If we do not reach an agreement, we agree to hire a mediator to help us come to a resolution of the problem before we will seek a resolution in court.

**3. Emergency medical decisions.** We agree that the parent who has the child at the time he/she suffers an emergency medical condition has authority to make any decision regarding emergency medical care. We agree to notify the other parent of the emergency as soon as possible.

**4. Day-to-day decisions.** We understand that whatever parent has physical custody of our children may make minor, day-to-day decisions regarding them and their care.

## Long-Distance Parenting

1. In the event that either of us decides to move out of the state or decides to move to a location in the state that makes our time-sharing arrangement impractical, we agree to revise our arrangement by discussing and reaching a time-sharing agreement prior to the parent's actual move.

2. The issues we agree to address include, but are not limited to, the following:

   a. Time-sharing

   b. Transportation details and cost allocation

   c. Procedure for ensuring that decision-making can be shared when required

   d. Procedure for sharing information about our children

3. If we cannot reach a long-distance parenting agreement on our own, we agree to consult with a mediator before we seek a resolution in court.

## Miscellaneous

**Mediation clause.** In the event any future dispute arises between us that we cannot resolve ourselves, we agree to enter into mediation before seeking a resolution in court.

**Requirement to obtain legal advice.** During mediation, we acknowledge that our mediator required that we seek legal advice concerning all issues arising in the context of this divorce proceeding. Each of us has considered the implications of this Agreement, has discussed it with our own legal counsel, and consider it to be fair and equitable

_____          _____
Signature                                      Signature

# 15
# *Finances and the Reality of Divorce*

The financial decisions you will make during your divorce process will have long-term consequences for your family. During a divorce, you may have to make decisions regarding the valuation and division of property and the payment of debts in addition to child support and spousal support.

It is important that both you and your spouse take time to understand your family's financial situation. You will make better decisions if both of you are knowledgeable about your financial affairs and possible settlement options.

The objective of a divorce proceeding is to arrive at a fair and equitable financial settlement. In order to reach such a settlement, the courts will require you to make a full and accurate disclosure of all assets and debts. This section contains financial worksheets to help you gather all relevant financial information and analyze your financial situation.

## *Property Division*

Under the law, property is divided into categories: real property and personal property. Real property includes real estate and improvements, such as a home or a commercial building. Personal property refers to everything else, including cash, investments, automobiles, recreational vehicles, furniture, personal effects, bank accounts, retirement accounts, stocks, bonds, business interests, and life insurance policies.

The court will make a fair and equitable division of property, dependent upon the principles of law established in your state for property division. Some states have community property laws while other states have laws that divide property based on principles of equity. Consult with your attorney regarding the property laws applicable in your state.

The first step in dividing property in a fair and equitable manner is to identify and value all assets. It is important for you and your spouse to agree on a valuation method.

Common methods of valuing your property include the following:

1. Fair market value—the price a buyer is willing to pay for an item of property and the price for which a seller is willing to sell.

2. Replacement value—the cost of replacing the item of property with a similar item.

3. Liquidation value—the amount of proceeds that would be realized if the item of property were quickly sold at a garage sale or "liquidation sale."

It is important to value your property in a consistent manner prior to dividing it. Otherwise, you and your spouse will have dissimilar perspectives and have difficulty reaching a fair property settlement.

## Options for Dividing Real Property

The following options are provided as suggestions only. Other options are possible. Please consult with your attorney regarding your unique financial situation.

### Land and House

1. Sell the real property and divide the proceeds in an equitable manner.

2. One spouse retains the right to reside in the home for a period of time, while the children are minors or until he/she remarries or becomes employed; thereafter, the property is sold and the proceeds divided.

3. One parent exchanges their half of the equity for other assets or cash of comparable value.

4. One of you purchases the home from the other.

5. One of you owns the home and rents the home to the other parent who resides there.

Consider the following in regard to real property:

- What is the market value of the real property or house?

- How should equity (the proceeds after closing costs, commissions, repairs, and tax liabilities are deducted) be calculated?

- Is it realistic for one of you to own the home after a divorce or is selling the home more practical?

- How should you share the responsibilities for fixing up, listing and advertising, and showing the house to potential buyers?

- Until the property is sold, who should be responsible for the mortgage payments, maintenance costs, taxes, and insurance?

- What are the income tax considerations?

- What is the cost of renting comparable housing?

- Have you sought the assistance of experts—accountants, attorneys, financial planners?

- If the property is not immediately sold, is refinancing available so as to remove one party from the loan obligation?

# Options for Dividing Personal Property

## Automobiles and Recreational Vehicles

1. Sell the automobiles or recreational vehicles and divide the proceeds.
2. Divide the vehicles, having any liabilities follow the property.
3. Trade your interest in a vehicle for another asset or cash equivalent.

When considering these and other options, review the following:

- The fair market value of a vehicle can most easily be determined by researching the blue book value of the vehicle.

- Is refinancing available to remove the name of one of the spouses from an underlying joint obligation?

- If such property has an underlying joint obligation, the court will typically require the party receiving the property to pay the debt and hold the other party harmless from the underlying obligation.

- Despite the fact that your decree may contain a hold harmless provision, a creditor can still seek payment from the joint obligor. This person must then seek recourse against their former spouse.

## Retirement Accounts

1. Each party retains their own account(s).
2. One party keeps his/her retirement account and buys out the other person's share with cash.

3. Trade the retirement account for another asset that is of comparable value, such as: equity in the house.

4. Divide the retirement account with a Qualified Domestic Relations Order, consulting with an experienced attorney.

As you consider these and other options, realize the following:

- Valuing retirement accounts is a technical process, requiring the assistance of experts.

- Often if money is withdrawn from a retirement account, income taxes and penalties may be assessed.

- Obtaining a Qualified Domestic Relations Order takes time and costs legal fees.

## Household Items (furniture, appliances, stereos, housewares)

In dividing your household items, consider the following:

- Determine the value of household items in a consistent manner.

- Decide on a fair procedure for dividing your personal property. For example: divide items each of you brought into the marriage, take turns choosing items, flip a coin.

- Consider trading household items for other assets of comparable value.

## Investments, Bank Accounts, Life Insurance Policies

As you divide investments, consider the following options:

- Divide your investments equally.

- Convert the ownership of an account or designate your children as the beneficiary of an insurance policy.

- Designate the purpose of a joint account to serve a need of your children. For example: convert a savings account to an educational, medical, or orthodontic account.

- Liquidate an investment to assist one spouse to set up another household or go to school.

## Debts

Your divorce will give you an opportunity to plan how debts will be paid. It is important for you to list all debts and assign payment responsibility. Debts should be divided in a fair and equitable manner. If debts are owed jointly, delays in payment may result in negative credit reports for both of you. This chapter contains a financial worksheet to help you to divide the payment responsibility of your debts.

# Spousal Support or Alimony

Courts are empowered to order one spouse to pay spousal support or alimony to the other spouse. A court will determine spousal support in connection with its decisions on custody, child support, property settlements, and debt divisions.

## History

Spousal support laws have a long history and have evolved according to societal attitudes. Traditionally, spousal support is awarded on the basis of financial need or for equitable reasons. Generally, spousal support is not awarded as a penalty against the payor spouse. Spousal support laws typically recognize a post-marital duty of support and maintenance for the purpose of preventing the payee spouse from becoming a public charge.

## Amount

Laws and judges have varying views regarding the amount and duration of spousal support. You should consult with an attorney for details about the law in your state regarding this subject.

In determining the amount of spousal support the court will either refer to guidelines adopted by the state legislature or consider a variety of factors including the following:

- The social position and standard of living of each party before the marriage.
- The respective ages of the parties.
- What each may have given up for the marriage.
- What money or property each brought into the marriage.
- The physical and mental health of the parties.
- The relative ability, training, and education of the parties.
- The duration of the marriage.
- The present income of the parties and the property acquired during the marriage and owned either jointly or by either of them at the time of the divorce.
- How property was acquired and the efforts of each in doing so.

- Children reared, their present ages, and obligations to the children or help which may be expected by the children.
- The present age and life expectancy of each of the parties.
- The happiness and pleasure (or lack of it) experienced during the marriage.
- Any extraordinary sacrifices, devotion, or care which may have been given to the other spouse.
- The present standard of living and needs of each.

Despite these considerations, courts are aware of certain realities. Often it is not economically possible for a court to award spousal support that enables a spouse to continue their standard of living when one household is divided into two. Consequently, courts will look closely at the payor spouse's ability to pay.

The length of the marriage is an important factor that is closely examined. Courts are less likely to award spousal support where the marriage is one of short duration and the spouse seeking support is employable. The longer the marriage, the more likely it is that one of the spouses has foregone employment opportunities in comparison to the other. Consequently, spousal support may be equitable under the circumstances.

Strong public policy concerns favor a court imposing an alimony award to assist a dependent spouse to become self-sufficient. In some cases, this may require a higher level of support payments at first while education, training, or job experience is obtained.

The court may award different types of spousal support. Rehabilitative alimony is typically of short duration and awarded to assist a spouse to readjust, obtain training and education, or to obtain employment. Long-term or permanent alimony is typically awarded when the marriage was one of long duration and the parties have significantly disparate earning capacities.

The court is also willing to consider all special circumstances and factors in determining the amount and duration of spousal support. For example, a court will make equitable adjustments in a case where one spouse made a direct contribution to the other's education or professional success. A court is also sensitive to health problems which reduce the spouse's earning capacity or increase financial need.

Federal tax laws require that the payee spouse declare spousal support payments as income. The payor spouse is entitled to deduct spousal support payments.

## *Options for Spousal Support*

Before determining the level of spousal support, it is important for you to project future monthly living expenses in order to see what amount of money is necessary to meet future needs.

You may creatively design a spousal support agreement that serves to accomplish clear objectives. For example, one party may pay a level of spousal support until their spouse completes school, training, or obtains a job.

You should consult with an accountant regarding the relative tax consequences and look at all options to maximize your income and lower your tax liabilities. The amount of money received by one spouse may be characterized as either spousal support or a property settlement, depending upon desired tax consequences or other considerations. It is important to characterize this money in careful consultation with your attorney and accountant.

# Financial Worksheets

The following worksheets are provided to assist you in understanding your current financial situation and in making fair and equitable settlement decisions.

**1. Gross monthly income.**

| | FATHER | MOTHER | CHILDREN |
|---|---|---|---|
| Salary and wages<br>(include commissions, bonuses, and royalties) | | | |
| Pensions and retirement | | | |
| Social Security | | | |
| Disability and unemployment | | | |
| Public Assistance<br>(AFDC payments, welfare) | | | |
| Child support/previous | | | |
| Dividends and interest | | | |
| Rents | | | |
| All other sources | | | |
| **Totals** | | | |

**2. Itemized monthly deductions from gross income.**

| | FATHER | MOTHER | CHILDREN |
|---|---|---|---|
| Federal income taxes | | | |
| State income taxes | | | |
| Social Security (FICA) | | | |
| Medical insurance | | | |
| Other insurance | | | |
| Union dues | | | |
| Retirement or pension fund | | | |
| Savings and/or 401K plan | | | |
| Credit Union | | | |
| Other | | | |
| **Total** | | | |
| **Net Monthly Income** | | | |

| | | ITEM | VALUE |
|---|---|---|---|
| I. | | Business Interest | Approximate value less indebtedness |
| | | Name | |
| | | Ownership Interest | $ |
| | | Type of Business | |
| | | | |
| J. | | Other assets | Value |
| | | | $ |
| | | | $ |
| | | | $ |

## Expenses of Creating a Two Home Family

A realistic budget can evaluate monthly expenses and help divorcing couples assess the costs of setting up two new households. The following worksheet has been designed with the intent of showing the expected amount of each parent's expenses after a separation or divorce.

## Monthly Expenses (Post Divorce)

| | Father's Home | Mother's Home |
|---|---|---|
| Number of children in household (primary residence) | | |
| Mortgage payments: | | |
| Principal | | |
| Interest | | |
| Property taxes | | |
| Property insurance | | |
| Rent payments | | |
| Maintenance/Home Repair Expenses | | |
| Furniture/Appliance Maintenance | | |
| Utilities | | |
| Water/garbage/sewer | | |
| Electricity | | |
| Heating Fuel/Natural Gas | | |
| Cable | | |
| Grounds maintenance | | |
| Telephone | | |
| Housekeeper | | |
| Food (include eating out) | | |
| Clothing | | |
| Laundry/dry cleaning | | |
| Medical costs | | |

# *Monthly Expenses (Post Divorce)*

| | Father's Home | Mother's Home |
|---|---|---|
| Dental costs | | |
| Eye care/glasses | | |
| Mental health care (include therapists, other professionals) | | |
| Prescriptions | | |
| Personal grooming/hair care | | |
| Recreation: | | |
|    Clubs/social obligations | | |
|    Vacation savings | | |
|    Summer Camp | | |
|    Allowances for children | | |
|    Entertainment | | |
| Education/Self Improvement: | | |
|    Magazines/newspapers | | |
|    Records/books | | |
|    Tuition/classes | | |
| Insurance/retirement: | | |
|    Life insurance premiums | | |
|    Accident/disability | | |
|    Retirement accounts | | |
| Charitable contributions | | |
| Child care | | |
| Child and spousal support payment from prior marriage | | |
| Incidentals: | | |
|    Gifts for children | | |
|    Gifts for family members | | |
|    Miscellaneous gifts | | |
|    Pet care | | |
| Transportation costs: | | |

# Monthly Expenses (Post Divorce)

| | Father's Home | Mother's Home |
|---|---|---|
| Automobile loan repayment | | |
| Automobile insurance | | |
| Automobile fuel and oil | | |
| Automobile repairs allowance | | |
| Automobile registration, license expense, etc. | | |
| Bus passes/carpool payments | | |
| Savings accounts | | |
| | | |
| | | |
| | | |
| Bank charges | | |
| Debt payments: | | |
| | | |
| | | |
| | | |
| Other miscellaneous expenses: | | |
| | | |
| | | |
| TOTAL: | | |

# Part III

Elizabeth Hickey, MSW

*No longer side by side*
*But we can see eye to eye*
*Together we stand apart*
*Somewhere in this space between us*
*We are . . . HEALING HEARTS*

*Michelle Linford*

# 16
## Medicine for the Heart

*Heal your heart, your head can wait.*
*It's your heart that is hurting now.*
*Your heart can't wait.*
*Once your heart is healed,*
*You can take time for your head,*
*Filling it with new thoughts,*
*Perspectives and directions.*
*But when you have a hurting heart,*
*It needs your love now.*

Although my co-author and I had worked in the professional arena of divorce for years, no schooling or professional experience prepared us for the pain of our own marital break-ups. Nothing prepares you for the kind of pain resulting from the reality of divorce and the unavoidable losses divorce brings.

## The Pain of Rejection

The media gives us stories of courtroom shootings, violence, and desperate parents kidnapping their children. What drives such rage?

One answer lies in the experience of feeling rejected. At the core of divorce, one person is rejecting another. One spouse is saying to the other, "You are not meeting my needs and I must end our relationship." The hearer of this message typically responds with shock and disbelief: "What? What's wrong? Sure, we have problems like everyone else. But we can work them out. You can't mean that you do not want *me* anymore!"

In all the hurt and confusion, the rejector is saying, "That's exactly what I mean; I don't want you anymore. I want a divorce. I want a life apart from you, but a life with my children nevertheless."

If you are the rejected, your first reaction might be, "No way. Because you don't want me, you can't have anything connected to me—my children, my money, or my concern for your needs or feelings. Why should I make it easy for you? After all, you have disrupted my life, stolen my dreams, hurt my children, and broken my heart."

This reaction comes from the heart of one devastated by a romantic wound. The romantic wound of a heart broken in a divorce hurts severely.

## The Guilt of the Rejector

The spouse choosing to end the marriage usually appears to be stronger than the rejectee but carries a heavy burden of guilt. If you are the rejector you are probably delivering a rejecting message in order to be true to your values. Somewhere along the road your feelings and perspectives changed. Usually you, the rejector, do not intend to inflict pain on the rejected. Rather, you are reaching down inside yourself and deciding to embark on a new road that allows for congruency of heart, mind, and soul.

Although there is a certain nobility in being true to your heart, the price of that nobility is costly in the context of a divorce. The rejector carries the burden of betraying another's expectation of marital security and commitment. In addition, you as the rejector must witness the pain your children experience as the family falls apart. It's extremely difficult to make changes when you know that these very changes cause pain to the ones you love.

Whether you are the rejector, or the rejected, or you both arrived at the decision simultaneously, one thing is clear: both hearts need healing if the family is to heal. If one person stays hurt and bitter, the family, in particular the children, will also feel this pain. What parent would intentionally inflict pain on their children? Very few—but when a heart is left unhealed, the pain directly touches the child. You owe it to yourself, you owe it to your child, and you owe it to your future partner to own and process your pain in order for your heart to heal.

Buried pain always surfaces, often not even in the same arena where it began. To be in control you need your heart, mind, and soul healed from the wounds of the past, and free to live in the present and embrace the future with hope.

Consider that life is a process of evolving and that all of your experiences can bring you higher awareness. Each of your experiences can increase your awareness level. Wisdom learned from heartache can be profound.

As I allowed myself to forgive my former husband and myself for each of our contributions to the divorce, I was freeing myself from the past. In the process, I allowed myself to open to possibilities for the future. But to be sure the last ten years taught me lessons that I could use and build on, I took quite a bit of time to reflect on what I would have done differently. Hindsight is very clear and while it can't change the past, it can be helpful for organizing thoughts, intentions, and choices for the future. I learned several lessons from my past which I hope to apply to future relationships.

## Greater Desire to Compromise

There is no education like adversity.

—Disraeli

Previously, I thought that if I wasn't genuinely interested in something, I would be a hypocrite if I acted as though I were just to please my partner. Now I know that sharing interests is an important aspect of a relationship. Spending quality time together builds a bond and closeness. I learned that sometimes I became so busy defending my identity that I didn't realize I might develop an interest in something outside my world. Ironic as it is, some of my former husband's interests that I forcefully resisted have now surfaced as genuine hobbies for me.

## Greater Spontaneity

Another lesson I learned is that spontaneity is important to keeping a relationship alive and thriving. My husband used to want to make love at what seemed to be inopportune times and places and my resistance put a damper on things. In the future I will be more open to being in the moment and not needing to have control. Being open to the moment and letting passion fill me will touch many other areas of my life with enthusiasm and spontaneity of spirit.

## Greater Appreciation

Not taking each other for granted is another important lesson. When couples are dating, they recognize the value of dressing up and having a nice appearance. During the marriage, probably at some point after the arrival of children, we tend to get rather relaxed about what we let our partner see. Maybe it's because we know our spouse has seen the worst of us, and is still around, so we get even more relaxed about it. Physical attractiveness is an important part of a strong relationship, and I will give it it's due attention next time.

I could go on and on with my lessons, but the important thing is that we all learn different things from our different relationships. What we do with what we learn is up to us.

Write down some of the lessons you may have learned from your experiences so far. Put the date next to them, because you might be surprised how they could change as you move along.

Being open to the future means not being afraid to acknowledge what you have learned. Finding a way to apply hard-earned wisdom will be a satisfying experience. Having confidence in yourself to go out and mingle in the world is important because you need to create opportunities for yourself.

I can write all this easily now, because I have moved through it and am free. But I can assure you that the road getting here was not easy. It involved heartache, sweat, and tears. It took a willingness to be open to feeling the pain, dealing with it, and making deliberate choices, as opposed to simply reacting to it.

And the bonus is that I feel stronger and more capable than I have ever felt. I experienced heartache that I could previously not have imagined, and I survived it. We all have resilience within us and when put to the test, we can draw on that. When it's all said and done, peace—and even joy—comes again in the morning.

We sincerely wish you well on your journey of healing. At times it will be very painful, but just knowing that the passage of pain leads you toward a healthier heart should encourage your motivation to let go and allow the healing to occur. The following statements were written to help you connect with that higher part of yourself that will take care of you and heal you during these challenging days.

All people are connected by the infinite wisdom that lives in each and every heart.

# *Healing Statements*

People can go in different directions and still have a relationship.

Conflict does not have to be destructive. Well-managed conflict creates a climate of growth.

What you resist will persist.

Changes bring about some things I like and some things I don't like. I can choose how I will respond to each change. My power of choice directs my outcome.

What others choose to do is not my responsibility. I can only be responsible for what I can control.

When I nurture me, I am indirectly nurturing my children. I bring a happier heart to them when I take care of myself.

What I feel, I can heal.

What I feel, my children will also feel through me. It's up to me to resolve the emotions that are not in my best interest. I can reach a place where I can forgive and move forward freely.

Every day brings a fresh opportunity to choose again.

Staying angry will hurt me more than anyone else. It is up to me to honestly and effectively deal with my legitimate anger in a way that supports my growth, as well as my children's growth.

When problems arise, I need to remind myself that emotions are not an expression of an intention. I may want to react in rage but my intention is to regulate my reaction in a way that supports my well-being.

Divorce is an individual walk. No one can do it for me. Others may support me, but ultimately, I will triumph through my own inner resources and strength.

My inner resources are great. I will dig deep in times of trouble.

All roads lead to the heart.

If I feel guilty, I will examine it and determine the source of my guilt. If there is something I can do to alleviate it, and I choose to do so, I will do it. If another has tried to make me feel guilty, I will examine whether it is best for me to accept this or reject it. Do I owe others an apology for anything? If so, what will I do about this? My growth will be supported if I am not tripped up in guilt, but rather if I apply past lessons to making wiser choices today.

I will make mistakes along the way. I can always apologize and start anew. If someone can't accept my apology, I will try another way of apologizing. Eventually, the apology will be heard even if the person has trouble accepting it.

## A Glimpse of Peace

I sometimes get a glimpse of peace
Like wings up in the sky.
So high above and out of reach
I watch as they pass by.

In my soul I long to fly,
But the confusion and the pain
Capture me and hold me
Like a heavy iron chain.

Memories of arguments,
All the anger in my heart. . .
Guilt, fear, and hostility
Are tearing me apart.

I feel frozen and afraid to move,
I cannot see a way,
To get past the painful problems
That block me every day.

I need a vision that is clear
So I can see ahead,
And choose a path that I can trust
To be positive instead.

I want to feel myself grow strong
After all that I've been through,
And have the strength and confidence
To start my life anew.

I need another glimpse of peace
Beyond the pain.
I have to see the happy times
And things that I can gain.

I'm learning how to rise up
From heartache and despair,
To focus on the future
And the happiness that's there.

# The Give and Take of Relationships

Consider that society systematically programs people to expect and appreciate instant gratification. It is important to remind yourself that relationships naturally create occasional frustrations and inconveniences.

Consider the businessman who leaves his house at 6:30 A.M. in order to get a jump on the day. He sends faxes from the mobile fax machine in his car, gets on the phone and calls the east coast (taking advantage of the time difference), arrives at his office to find coffee and snacks waiting for him, and then organizes his day according to his priorities. He has his staff handle things that bog him down, his secretary screens his calls, and he chooses the items that require his attention.

After a full and productive day, he sets out for home. Listening to the radio, he hears a pizza advertisement that tells him "you earned it—you deserve it—order the best pizza around," and he happens to agree. Upon arriving home, he is still mentally debating what to order on his pizza, when he notices that two of his children are standing in the driveway looking rather frantic. They promptly inform him that they need rides to lessons because their car pool didn't show up, the sprinkler system has gone haywire and needs to be shut off, and Mom came home from work early with the flu. This is not exactly what he dreamed about on the way home. Is anything at home in his control, or is he being directed by the circumstances around him?

The above situation could happen in various forms to most people—male or female. Once the decision is made to start a family, your freedom of choice is definitely affected. There will be those who argue that freedom is a state of mind, and if you feel free, then you are free, regardless of what is imposed on you. To a certain degree, I agree with that theory. But the reality of the situation is that bringing children into this world demands sacrifice, compromise, flexibility, commitment, and a willingness to serve others. Without it, children are doomed. Parenting is tough enough with the support of two parents, why should one parent have to do it on their own?

Promoting a sense of responsibility that goes with bringing a child into this world will improve the world for everyone. People must recognize that financial child support is only one aspect of raising a child, and that active emotional, spiritual, moral, and physical support are essential to promoting a child's sense of well-being.

Relationships, in whatever form, require give and take. The advertising world tries to make us believe that we deserve it all. We've worked hard, and after all, we should expect more. We suggest that we should expect a slightly lesser degree than we are willing to give, so that our spirits can remember the importance of humility. And if we are given a lot, then we should give a lot. If

The sea of life
  brings many waves;
    some we ride on,
      others we break with.

But through it all
  we emerge,
    we gasp for breath,
      and swim again.

The tide may change,
  but the rhythm
    of the heart
      always beats for love.

we feel that we haven't been given a lot, then we should examine what obstacles exist in our lives to prevent us from receiving. What might we do to change the flow of energy in our lives? What are we willing to do?

Reality tells us that there are many hurting adults and children in our world. The rage, the violence, the revenge, the abuse. . . are all signs of trouble. When a child grows up under these types of circumstances, what are they being taught? How can we also teach them about the good to be found inside people, the places within that inspire kind deeds, and the human bonding that goes far beyond family blood lines? What are each of us willing to do to ensure that children are taught that hope and goodness are not just ideals to be taken lightly, but that each and every person possesses the same potential for love and for good deeds?

Environmental situations will vary forever, needs of the heart will never change. What it needed yesterday, it still needs today, and will need tomorrow. *Unconditional love. Unconditional love. Unconditional love.*

Once a heart is wounded, it needs to be healed if it is to be free. If your heart is healing, what will you do to contribute to the healing of another heart? The love within our hearts unites us and always will.

In peace and love,

*Elizabeth Hickey*     *Elizabeth Dalton*

> The heart holds healing plans
> Waiting for our permission
>   to release
>   to mourn
>   to lift
> To higher places
> Where eagles fly.

## The Eagle's Wisdom

I looked and saw an eagle soaring through a stormy sky
It didn't stop or hesitate or pause to wonder why.
It simply flew upon the winds as every eagle must
And moved about the air with confidence and trust.

The eagle's flight inspires my hope
I know that I can always cope.
When storm clouds come and winds blow fast
My faith can lift me 'till they're past.

I felt myself uplifted to new heights again today
I rose up and stayed much longer than I did just yesterday.
Gliding high above the forest, I could see across the trees
And get a larger vision of all the possibilities.

Starting in my center it traveled on and through.
I could feel contentment and power as it grew.
The strength of peace and trusting in life's gentle helping hand
Lifts and guides me to a better path across the land.

The eagle didn't fight the storm. He spread his mighty wings.
He let its fury lift him up in ever rising rings.
High above the lightning, the thunder and the cold
The sunlight touched his feathers and turned them into gold.